IN-LAWS,
OUTLAWS,
and Everyone in Between

OTHER BOOKS AND AUDIO BOOKS
BY KATHRYN JENKINS GORDON:

Colorful Characters in Mormon History

Butch Cassidy and Other Mormon Outlaws of the Old West

Keeping It Real: A Tribute to Everyday Moms

Scripture Study Made Simple: The Book of Mormon

The Essential Book of Mormon Companion

My Redeemer Lives

A Father's Greatest Gift

The First Nativity

IN-LAWS,
OUTLAWS,
and Everyone in Between
More Colorful Characters in Mormon History

Kathryn Jenkins Gordon

Covenant Communications, Inc.

Published by Covenant Communications, Inc.
American Fork, Utah

Printed in the United States of America
First Printing: May 2016

20 19 18 17 16   10 9 8 7 6 5 4 3 2 1

ISBN-13: 978-1-52440-050-7

To Glenn, who encourages and supports and loves me. I wouldn't have found Olive Ann Oatman without you.

To my children on this side of the pond—Ryan, Jessica, Nicholas, and Melissa—who inspire me every single day to be better. Ed, we hope you hop on board soon.

And to my children in Australia and Germany—Darren, Nicole, John, Dan, Lena, Josh, Jess, and Cam. Love you all!

To my grandchildren—Brooklyn, Noah, Charlotte, Jake, Kiahna, and the little girl who's on her way—you are the sunshine in my life.

To Susan Easton Black, Mary Jane Woodger, Glenn Rawson, and Dennis Lyman, who ignited in me an unquenchable love for history.

To KSL's Doug Wright, who I am convinced is my biggest fan.

To the team at Covenant, who always believes in me.

And to my Heavenly Father, who sent me here with a gift for writing. He lifts and inspires and protects me and, with the Savior, is the source of all my hope.

Thanks to all of you.

CONTENTS

INTRODUCTION

COLORFUL.

Back in the days when the characters in this book were alive, it meant "interesting."

Today, Webster's defines it as "vigorous, spirited, dynamic," "presenting or suggesting vivid or striking scenes."

And when it comes to the ten men and five women featured in these pages, oh, boy—they are all of those things and more.

You'll find here a collection of some of the most colorful folks you'll ever come to know—even more colorful than the handful of flamboyant associates you're bound to find here and there in your own family tree, your ward, or your neighborhood. Because, face it: we all have those.

Keep in mind that *colorful* doesn't necessarily mean bad. Oh, there's no disputing that some of these characters were bad. In fact, a few were very, very bad (kind of like the little girl with the curl right in the middle of her forehead). You know, like killing-three-adventurers-and-burying-them-in-the-floor-of-the-local-meetinghouse bad. Like killing-a-prostitute-in-the-apartment-he-shared-with-the-full-time-missionaries bad. Like throwing-rocks-and-rotten-fruit-and-even-books-at-the-stake-president bad. (Okay, that's not as bad as *killing* someone, but it's still pretty bad.) Yep, there are some real whoppers scrambling across these pages.

But there are some colorful *and* good characters too. Like the spinster who boldly struck out all by herself and walked 251 miles to Kirtland so she could meet the Prophet Joseph Smith. Or the homesick soldier on an isolated Italian island who built a chapel from cigarettes. Or the Relief Society president who built a maternity hospital (not from cigarettes) and staffed it with volunteers so no more women would die in childbirth.

There's even a ghost or two among the ranks of these oddballs—or so say the folks who claim to have seen them.

All of the characters featured here were members of The Church of Jesus Christ of Latter-day Saints . . . or at least they were for a time. Some were asked to leave. Some, on the other hand, grabbed on to one dispute or another and left on their own. The record-breaker was the guy whose Church membership lasted a stunning *eight days* and who then spent the rest of his life, literally, haranguing and pestering every Mormon he could find.

One was kidnapped by Indians. One was married to Brigham Young. And some, of course, were faithful to the end (even when they shouldn't have been—you'll see what that means).

So pull up a chair, grab a snack, and dive in. You're sure to have a rip-roaring, knee-slapping good time!

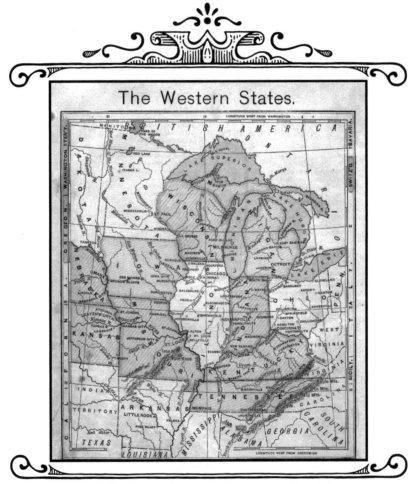

Map showing the territory where James Strang presided over his subjects. Believe it or not, as the title states, this was considered "the west" at the time.

JAMES STRANG
THE MAN WHO WOULD BE KING

As you undoubtedly know, a bit of chaos ensued following the martyrdom of the Prophet Joseph Smith regarding who would be the next Church president. After all, this was the first time the fledgling church had been faced with the succession question—and they clearly didn't expect it to happen so soon.

As you also undoubtedly know, there was quite a scuffle as one candidate after another stepped up to offer his services. But perhaps none were quite as peculiar as that of a relative newcomer to the scene—a man who had been a member of the Church for only *four months* at the time. His name was James Strang, and where he was concerned, things continued to get progressively more bizarre.

But before we look at all that, let's start at the beginning.

James—who was originally known as Jesse James Strang—was born on his father's farm in Scipio, New York, on March 21, 1813. He changed his name to James Jesse Strang when he became an adult. He was smack dab in the middle of the three children born to Clement and Abigail James Strang, people who had a good reputation in their community. His brother, David, was almost two years older, and his sister, Myraette (oh, golly), was five years younger.[1]

James wasn't exactly hale and hearty; in fact, he was a frail child who was often sick. After he died, someone found the beginning of an autobiography he had started to write, and talk about colorful: it was a diary written in a code that took more than a hundred years to decipher. (His own grandson Mark Strang, a banker in Long Beach, California, finally cracked the code.) Here's how James himself described his childhood:

> My infancy was a period of continual sickness and extreme suffering and I have understood that at one time I was so low as to be thought dead, and that preparations were made for my burial. All my early recollections are painful, and at this day I am utterly unable to comprehend the feeling of those who look back with pleasure on their infancy, and regret the rapid passing away of childhood. Till I had children of my own, happy in their infantile gambols, the recollection of those days produced a creeping sensation akin to terror.[2]

Doesn't exactly sound like the type of guy who would charge in, all guns blazing, and forcefully demand control—but just wait. Just wait.

Sickly though he might have been, he and his family led fairly run-of-the-mill lives for the time. His mother doted on him because of his frailty, but seemed a bit like a drill sergeant, demanding that he account for every minute he was out of her sight.[3] When he was three, his family moved to Hanover, New York, a few counties away.

James may have been sick, but he was apparently an exceptionally bright boy. He read extensively and went to a rural public school until he was twelve, which was more education than many got back then. However, things aren't always as they seem. In his autobiography, James said that "the terms were usually short, the teachers inexperienced and ill qualified to teach, and my health such as to preclude attentive study or steady attendance."

When all was said and done, he estimated that his actual time in a classroom totaled six months.[4]

James also complained that his teachers "not unfrequently turned me off with little or no attention, as though I was too stupid to learn and too dull to feel neglect." Pontificating in his diary, he remembers that he spent "long weary days . . . upon the floor, thinking, thinking, thinking. . . . My mind wandered over fields that old men shrink from, seeking rest and finding none till darkness gathered thick around and I burst into tears."[5]

What a riot . . . for him *and* his poor teachers.

He was enrolled for a time at New York's Fredonia Academy,[6] which boasted an enrollment of about two hundred and eventually became part of the State University of New York system.

According to his diary, he had some real regrets by the time he reached the ripe old age of nineteen. He had expected by then to be a general—or, at the very least, a member of the state legislature. You see, he had a plan mapped out in his quest for fame and glory,[7] and things weren't happening as quickly as he anticipated. Even at that young age, he intended to become a person of power that would "rival Caesar or Napolean."

But in case you think him too power-hungry, you should know the rest of the story: there was another side to James Strang. He also expressed in his diary his heartfelt desire to be of service to his fellow man—and he didn't know how that was going to happen to a penniless, unknown boy from upstate New York.

We're sure you're catching the irony of all this.

With all that stellar education in his pocket, James faced the dilemma of what to do for his livelihood. He knew one thing for sure: he didn't want to be a farmer, like his father. So he decided to practice law. He was admitted to the New York bar at the age of twenty-three and was subsequently admitted to other bars as he moved from one place to another.

In Hanover, James developed a real reputation for his persuasive public speaking and debating—but he also had a reputation for being restless.[8] A good part of that was undoubtedly due to the way he jumped with seeming careless abandon from one occupation to another: in addition to practicing law, he was at times a school teacher, politician, newspaper editor (the *Randolph Herald* and the *Daily Northern Islander*), county postmaster, temperance lecturer, and even Baptist minister. That, of course, was before he joined up with the Mormons.

At age twenty-three—the same year he was admitted to the New York bar—James married Mary Perce, the eighteen-year-old daughter of a Baptist minister. Lest you think the Baptist faith ran in the family, hear this: Mary's sister was married to a Mormon by the name of Moses Smith (no relative of the Prophet Joseph Smith). Mary's uncle, Benjamin Perce, was also a Mormon—and in 1843, when James moved to Burlington, Wisconsin, to be closer to family, Benjamin introduced James to the Church.

First, there were the relatives. Then there were two proselyting missionaries, who taught James the restored gospel. Early in 1844, James decided to take a trip to Nauvoo, Illinois, to meet the Prophet Joseph Smith. That did it: James quickly developed a fast friendship with the Prophet and was baptized by Joseph Smith himself in the unfinished font of the Nauvoo Temple on either February 24 or 25, 1844. Different sources disagree on the exact date, but the important thing is that he was baptized.

As generally happens, life changed dramatically for James after his baptism. On March 3, just days later, he was ordained an elder by Hyrum Smith. The Prophet then sent him to Wisconsin, where he was asked to establish a Mormon stake at the town of Voree. (Remember that name; it figures prominently in this story later on.) He was also asked to help scout out the area around Burlington, Wisconsin; persecution was mounting in Nauvoo, and some Church leaders were apparently considering relocating the faith's headquarters. James was only too happy to comply, and he sent leaders a favorable report at the end of May 1844.

A month later, on June 27, 1844, the Prophet was martyred in Carthage, Illinois.

And that's where things got dicey.

Before he died, Joseph Smith made his wishes clear: he told the Quorum of the Twelve that if he were to die, they were to take over the leadership of the Church.⁹ As president of the Quorum of the Twelve, Brigham Young seemed the logical choice as leader, and he stood ready to accept that assignment.

There was just one problem, and it was a major one: most of the Twelve, along with the First Presidency, were away on missions, many in the eastern United States. That left what looked like a leadership vacuum, and chaos ensued.

Practically before Church members could catch their breath, at least two additional contenders for the spot of president stepped forward. One was Sidney Rigdon. You remember him: the first counselor in the First Presidency. He claimed having received a vision that *he* was supposed to be the "guardian" of the Church— that no one was supposed to assume the role of prophet following Joseph Smith's death. But lots of folks who were milling around Nauvoo and wondering what to do were well aware that Rigdon had started to lose favor with Joseph Smith in the months before the Prophet's murder. No, they figured; *that* can't be right.

The other primary contender (among a handful of others) who immediately stepped up was none other than our boy James Strang, a convert of only four months. An obvious newcomer to the faith, James didn't possess any of the status or name recognition of Brigham Young or Sidney Rigdon—not to mention the leadership experience and knowledge of the gospel.

Let's face it: his prospects looked pretty shaky at first.

Not one to let any moss grow under his feet, James contended that *he* was, in fact, the real president of the Church. Just in case anyone doubted him, he had proof. And he was ready to present that proof—not to any of the Twelve, who had started returning to Nauvoo in response to the crisis, and not to the main body of the Church in Nauvoo. Instead, James convened a conference of his own in Florence, Michigan, on August 5, 1844. And *there* he first presented his "proof."

James had in his hand a "Letter of Appointment" dated June 18, 1844—just seven days before Joseph Smith was jailed at Carthage and nine days before he was martyred—and bearing a Nauvoo postmark. (Just so you know, that letter is currently owned by Yale University.) The letter was allegedly from Joseph Smith, naming Strang as his successor as president of the Church. It also said that the Church was to move its headquarters to Voree, Wisconsin. (There's that name again.)

It didn't stop there. James also claimed that on the day Joseph Smith died, an angel appeared and ordained James as Joseph's successor. As proof of the veracity of that claim, James produced a witness who said that even though James was 225 miles away from the scene of the Prophet's martyrdom, he told people the Prophet had died before the news was made public. (Don't let that rattle you; you'll learn a lot more about James Strang's "witnesses" a bit later.)

Response to the letter was mixed, as you can imagine. The presiding priesthood authority at the conference in Florence, Crandall Dunn, said the letter was a fraud. (Yale experts later said that while the postmark appears to be legitimate, Joseph Smith's alleged signature is definitely forged.) After examining the letter, the Twelve were unconvinced. Brigham Young said, "Every person acquainted with Joseph Smith, and his style of dictation and writing, might readily know that he never wrote nor caused to be written that letter to Strang."[10]

Strang insisted that the letter was legitimate and that he had been ordained by an angel.

The Twelve, which had convened in Nauvoo by August 6, summarily excommunicated him for that very claim.

Though James insisted that he had not received a fair or legitimate trial, the Twelve wasted no time in rapidly publishing a notice of his excommunication in the *Times and Seasons*.[11]

At that point, most people so publicly humiliated would slink out of town, their tail between their legs. But not James. Oh, no. He demanded that the Twelve had no right to sit in judgment of him because *he* was the real president of the Church.

Oh, my.

On August 8, 1844, the Twelve held a solemn assembly that became perhaps the most important in Church history. As the meeting started out, Sidney Rigdon blathered on for an hour and a half about his vision and his argument for appointing only a "guardian," not a president. His remarks put to rest, a truly amazing thing took place. You've heard all about it: as Brigham Young began to speak, the mantle of the Prophet Joseph Smith fell on him. Brigham Young looked like Joseph Smith (down to the very style of his clothes), sounded like Joseph Smith, and moved like Joseph Smith. Many in attendance jumped to their feet, so great was their astonishment.

Twenty-one-year-old Zina Diantha Huntington, who would later marry Brigham Young, wrote, "President Young was speaking. It was the voice of Joseph Smith—not that of Brigham Young. His very person was changed. . . . I closed my eyes. I could have exclaimed, I know that is Joseph Smith's voice! Yet I knew he had gone. But the same spirit was with the people."

For most people—and clearly for the Church leadership—the succession crisis was over. The Quorum of the Twelve, with Brigham Young as its president, assumed leadership of the Church, and Brigham Young became its prophet and president. Not long after, he began the process of shuttling the bulk of Joseph Smith's followers across the plains to the Utah Territory.

Not everyone went, of course. Sidney Rigdon, disaffected from the Church, took a much smaller group and went to Pennsylvania.

And that left James Strang. You see, a small and isolated group of people were still confused about who to follow. Go with Brigham Young? What about Sidney Rigdon? Capitalizing on that confusion and indecision, James Strang leaped in and went for the jugular. There was, after all, the business of that letter.

Believe it or not, despite all indications to the contrary, a number of people—including a handful of prominent Mormons—*initially* believed Strang's story and accepted the letter as legitimate. They included four of the witnesses of the Book of Mormon: Martin Harris, Hiram Page, and John and David Whitmer. He also convinced three Apostles—William Smith (the Prophet's brother), William E. McLellin, and John E. Page—as well as Nauvoo Stake President William Marks and

Bishop George Miller. William Smith later said that everyone in the Prophet's family other than the widows of Hyrum and Samuel Smith hitched their wagons to the star that was James Strang.

But don't be too concerned: most of these folks eventually regained their wits and abandoned James.

Despite that, his little flock began to grow, gathering in his designated headquarters in Voree, Wisconsin. James busied himself setting up his Church organization much as Joseph Smith had, requiring members to pay tithing and making plans to build a temple. He also said that heavenly messengers led him to two sets of inscribed plates (one in Michigan and another in Wisconsin), which he subsequently translated[12] using the biblical Urim and Thummim.

Sounding familiar?

James even came up with witnesses who were willing to validate his story about the plates. More about that later.

Strang then took it upon himself to excommunicate the Mormon Church's Quorum of the Twelve, even though they weren't members of *his* church. Bit of a power struggle, it seems.

At that point he penned a letter to John Taylor and Orson Hyde, challenging their authority and asking for what amounted to a showdown. Dated August 30, 1846, and sent from Philadelphia, the text read:

> Messrs. J. Taylor and Orson Hyde –
>
> Knowing from your public proceedings, as well as otherwise, that you, and others associated with you, claim the right, and are attempting to use the power of dictating all the affairs of the Church of Jesus Christ in all the world, not under the directions of the first presidency thereof, but independently; I suggest to you the propriety of publicly showing by what means you are authorized to act as leaders to said Church, and offer to publicly discuss

that question with you in this city, or any other proper place that will suit your convenience.

Your answer to this, left at the house of Jacob Gibson, on the N.E. corner of Third and Dock streets, near the post-office, will receive immediate attention.

Yours respectfully,

JAMES J. STRANG.[13]

Well, apparently John Taylor and Orson Hyde were having none of it. Their reply is an absolute classic:

Sir –

After Lucifer was cut off and thrust down to hell, we have no knowledge that God ever condescended to investigate the subject or right of authority with him.

Your case has been disposed of by the authorities of the Church, and being satisfied with our own power and calling, we have no disposition to ask whence yours came.

Yours respectfully,

ORSON HYDE,

JOHN TAYLOR.[14]

As he continued to establish his church, James copied some of the practices and principles of the Mormon Church . . . sort of. One was a communal living system, very similar to the United Order, in which members consecrated all their possessions to the church. He also instituted baptism for the dead—but not just anyone could sign up. He required that the person wanting to do the baptism receive a revelation (angelic appearances, dreams, and so on) if the baptism was being done for anyone other than a close relative. And he taught eternal marriage—though, of course, the marriage didn't have to be performed in a temple (since they had none); it *did* have to be performed by an apostle, high priest, elder, or priest.

You should know that James *did* try to build a temple, but his plans fell flat. His followers didn't support the notion, and the church was too poor to build such an edifice even if everyone had hopped on board. Nothing like the LDS endowment ever existed, and obviously there was no temple marriage.

Speaking of marriage, James sanctioned plural marriage in his church (which was interesting, because he was initially vehemently opposed to it), but there were some strings attached: a man wasn't to take a new wife if he couldn't afford her, he couldn't dump one woman to marry another, nor was he to take a new wife "to vex" the ones he already had. Current wives could speak up and even object to a new marriage, but they did not have the power to veto it. (One would wonder why they should speak up, then. . . .) In all of his rhetoric, he claimed that plural marriage was to benefit the woman: she could pick the very best husband possible, even if he was already married.

That about wraps up the similarities between the Strangites (as James's followers became known) and the Latter-day Saints.

But oh, were there differences.

Let's start with the priesthood. He too had the Melchizedek (which he called "the priesthood of an endless life") and the Aaronic (dubbed simply "the priesthood of life") priesthoods. There were two offices in his Melchizedek priesthood—priests and apostles—but those were subdivided into "degrees." The priests were subdivided into high priests (called "sons of God," which included patriarchs) and elders. The apostles were subdivided into four degrees: the president of the church (who was referred to as a king), the president's counselors (who were called viceroys), the twelve apostles (called "Princes in His Kingdom forever"), and a quorum of evangelists.

Then there was the Strangite Aaronic Priesthood, which contained three "degrees"—priests, teachers, and deacons. You might think that's sounding pretty familiar, but here the differences become even more pronounced.

Priests consisted of sacrificators (the guys who killed the animals for sacrifice) and singers. The office of singers could include women, but they were specifically prohibited from killing the sacrifices. Not sure what they were singing about.

Teachers were subdivided into five degrees: rabboni, rabbi, doctor, ruler, and teacher. Women were also ordained to the office of teacher. There might have been a very practical reason for that: not only were they supposed to teach spiritual matters, but they were supposed to open and run and teach in schools. Aha.

Then there were the three degrees of deacons: marshals, stewards, and ministers. They were to be keepers of the king's prisons and courts.

James not only ordained women to two offices in the Aaronic Priesthood, but invited them to lecture in his School of the Prophets.

You probably figured out by now that James instituted animal sacrifice. Official church policy said the sacrifices were primarily to compensate for sin, but instead they were mostly used as part of celebrations—especially to commemorate James's coronation as king. Every household, even the most poverty-stricken among them, was to sacrifice a clean heifer, lamb, or dove.

James had a contorted view of agency: he emphasized that every person was to "willingly" conform to God's laws and character. The Sabbath was observed on Saturday. Followers were expected to be devoted conservationists, and each was to plant and maintain a grove of trees on his property.

James even departed a bit (okay, a lot) from Christianity in general. He accepted the Ten Commandments, but added one: "Thou shalt love thy neighbor as thyself." And he rejected the notion of a virgin birth when it came to Jesus, whom he claimed was the "natural-born son" of Mary and Joseph. He believed that Jesus was basically "adopted" as God's son at birth and had been chosen before time began to be the Savior of mankind. Only after "proving" himself to God by living a perfectly sinless life, taught James Strang, was Jesus able to atone for the sins of mankind.

As for God, James had some different ideas there, too. He preached that God could not do *all* things any more than the rest of us can. And while not actually using the word *evolution*, he said that God had been working through eons of time to refine things and make them better.

Now that you see what the Strangites were all about, let's examine that polygamy issue a bit more closely. At first, as we mentioned, James was vehemently opposed to polygamy, and so, as a result, were the Strangites. In fact, some of the early members he attracted were people who had disagreed with the Mormon Church when it came to plural marriage.

In 1848, James mysteriously changed his position on polygamy. It was a sudden and fairly disquieting about-face for a lot of people, including James's wife Mary Perce, who was "more than mildly disturbed" about her husband wanting to practice plural marriage. And it had a ripple effect among his church members as well. The band who had latched onto James because they hated polygamy unlatched themselves just as quickly. In fact, William Smith—Joseph Smith's brother, who had supported James from the beginning—bailed and went on to help establish the Reorganized Church of Jesus Christ of Latter Day Saints (now called the Community of Christ).

James announced the new policy of allowing polygamy in 1848, but he didn't actually marry his first plural wife until a year later on July 13, 1849, when he wed nineteen-year-old Elvira Eliza Field. And here's a colorful little tidbit: for the first year or more of their marriage, she disguised herself as a man and claimed she was "Charlie J. Douglas," James's nephew. Forget colorful. That is just plain weird.

Three years later, on January 19, 1852, he married thirty-one-year-old Betsy McNutt. Remember wife number one, Mary, who was "more than mildly disturbed" about her husband practicing polygamy? Two years after James married Betsy, Mary left. Things are a bit murky here: some say *she* left, some say she was *asked* to leave. Whichever it was, she left, but remained legally married to James until his death.

James's fourth wife was nineteen-year-old Sarah Adelia Wright, whom he married on July 15, 1855. From her, we get most of our information about the Strang polygamy setup. She reported that while James was "mild-spoken" and kind to his family, his word was law. You can read between the lines there. And here's a bit of a delightful irony: following James's death, Sarah married a man named Dr. Wing; she subsequently divorced him because *he* became interested in polygamy. We guess she'd had enough.

James's fifth and final wife was Sarah's cousin, eighteen-year-old Phoebe Wright, who was brought into the fold on October 27, 1855. According to their daughter, Eugenia, Phoebe started feeling "dissatisfied" with polygamy just a few months into the marriage, though she continued to love James "devotedly" all her life, even though he was dead less than a year after their marriage.

Like the Mormons, the Strangites had scriptures—two sets of them, to be precise. They were, claimed James, his translations of supposedly long-lost works that contained important doctrine.

The first was the Voree Record, sometimes called the "Voree Plates" or the "Rajah Manchou Plates." They consisted of a miniscule—roughly one and a half by three inches, small enough to fit in the palm of your hand—set of three brass plates. James claimed the plates held the final testimony of a man named "Ralph Machou of Vorito," who had lived in the area centuries earlier and had recorded his testimony for posterity.

James's account of how he found the plates rings familiar to Latter-day Saints: he said he was led by a heavenly messenger to the site where the plates were buried. But that's where the similarity ends. James towed four witnesses along with him, and they allegedly helped dig up the plates, which were illustrated and inscribed on both sides. James then claims to have translated and published the plates.

Modern-day Strangites (there are still about two hundred of them) say that two modern scholars affirmed that the text on the plates seemed to be from a genuine but unknown language. That was never verified. The plates disappeared around 1900, and no one seems to know where they are.

What about the witnesses? We know that some of the witnesses to the Book of Mormon subsequently left the Mormon Church. But remember that not one of them, even after leaving the Church, ever denied having seen the plates (and, for some, the angel).

Not so with James Strang and his four witnesses who purportedly help him dig up the Voree plates. In fact, according to Mormon scholar Daniel C. Peterson,[15] Caleb P. Barnes, one of the supposed witnesses, told ex-Strangite and former church leader Isaac Scott that he and James had actually *fabricated* the plates. According to Scott:

> [The men] made the "plates" out of Ben [Perce]'s old kettle and engraved them with an old saw file, and . . . when completed they put acid on them to corrode them and give them an ancient appearance; and that to deposit them under the tree, where they were found, they took a large auger . . . which Ben [Perce] owned, put a fork handle on the auger and with it bored a long slanting hole under a tree on "The Hill of Promise," as they called it, laying the earth in a trail on a cloth as taken out, then put the "plates" in, tamping in all the earth again, leaving no trace of their work visible.[16]

Hang on—Ben Perce? You remember him. He was James's first wife's uncle, the one who helped introduce James to the Mormon Church. And now here is James, using Ben's old kettle to manufacture the plates and his large auger to bury them. Wild.

According to Peterson:

> Among the many who saw [the plates] was Stephen Post, who reported that they were brass and, indeed, that they resembled the French brass used in familiar kitchen kettles. "With all the faith & confidence that I could exercise," he wrote, "all that I could realize was that Strang made the plates himself, or at least that it was possible that he made them." One source reports that most of the four witnesses to the

Rajah Manchou plates ultimately repudiated their testimonies.[17]

Ouch. Not so much like Joseph Smith's experience after all.

The other set of scriptures James Strang gave his church—and the one they still use today—was the Book of the Law of the Lord, which he claims to have transcribed from the Plates of Laban. Yes, *those* plates of Laban, the ones mentioned in the Book of Mormon. James said they consisted of eighteen brass plates, about seven and a half by nine inches in size. While they were first mentioned in 1849, he did not show them to witnesses until 1851. At that time seven witnesses saw the plates but experienced nothing "miraculous." Their testimonies are published in the preface to the book.

James told his followers that the book was the original law given to Moses, as mentioned in 2 Chronicles 34:14–15. When he finished the translation in 1851, the book consisted of 84 pages. In 1856, shortly before he died, he published a greatly expanded version that had bulked up to 350 pages. It's the book that contained that "addition" to the Ten Commandments. . . .

How about the witnesses to the plates of Laban? One, Samuel P. Bacon, eventually denied the inspiration of James's church and "denounced it as mere 'human invention.' Another, Samuel Graham, later claimed that he had actually assisted Strang in the creation of the plates."[18]

And here's how that came down:[19]

George Adams—James's first counselor, who would later crown him "king"—said that James asked him to dress in a long, white robe soaked in phosphorous to make him look like an angel. Samuel Graham said that he and James then fabricated the plates of Laban. Samuel Bacon, who had been one of the witnesses, later discovered fragments of the plates hidden in James's ceiling while he was doing repairs to the house; realizing the ruse, he left the church.

In his letter to Joseph Smith III, Chauncy Loomis was pretty harsh about the things that happened:

At this time George [Adams] was gone from the island on some business. When he returned and

saw how things were going he left the island with
his family. I saw him and wife after this on Mack-
inaw Island. He said to me, "Brother Loomis,
I always thought you to be an honest man, but
you are like poor dog Tray; you have been caught
in bad company, and now my advice to you is
to leave the island, for I tell you Strang is not a
prophet of God. I consider him to be a self-con-
fessed imposter. Strang wanted me to get a couple
of bottles of phosphoros [*sic*] and dress myself in
a long white robe and appear on the highest summit on the island, called Mount Pisgah, break the
bottles, make an illumination and blow a trum-
pet and disappear so that he might make it appear that an angel had made them a visit; that
it might beget faith in the Saint" . . . I speak of
these things that you may see how we were Strang
led. . . . Bro. Samuel Graham, I think, president
of the Twelve, declared that he and Strang made
those plates that Strang claimed to translate the
Book of the Law from. But they in the first place
prepared the plates and coated them with bees-
wax and then formed the letters and cut them
in with a pen knife and then exhibited them to
the rest of the Twelve. . . . Bro. Samuel Bacon
says that in repairing Strang's house he found hid
behind the ceiling the fragments of those plates
which Strang made the Book of the Law from.
He turned infidel and left the island.[20]

While in Voree, James was attracting more people to his faith
all the time, and before long the little hamlet was bursting at the
seams. There simply was no more room for all the people who
were arriving and wanting to be counted among the faithful.
In 1847—the same year Brigham Young left for Utah with the

vanguard company of pioneers—James Strang had a migration of his own, moving his church and its members to Beaver Island, Wisconsin, on the northern end of Lake Michigan.

As far as islands go, Beaver was a relatively small one: thirteen miles long and three to six miles wide, depending on what part of the island you were measuring. Its total size was about fifty-six square miles. As small as it was, it boasted seven lakes and two streams. Mostly flat and sandy, it did have several areas of thick forest. The climate was not the greatest: hot and humid in the summer, severely cold in the winter. (Today, the state owns a sizable part of the island, and approximately 650 people still live there.)

The Strangites established a town they named Saint James. It's still the most populous township on the island, and one that now also takes in a handful of tiny islands in Lake Michigan.

By June 1850, James's followers on Beaver Island totaled close to twelve thousand, and it was time for him to assert his authority. The Book of the Law, one of the two scriptural books he published, made clear that the church leader was to be king. (Incidentally, he claimed that Joseph Smith himself had been secretly crowned "king of the Kingdom of God" before his martyrdom. It must have been a *really big* secret, since no one but James had ever heard of it.)

And so on July 8, 1850, James Strang was officially made king in a coronation ceremony in Saint James witnessed by about three hundred of his followers. His counselor and prime minister—an actor named George J. Adams—crowned him with a tin crown adorned with a cluster of glass stars on the front. James's costume for the coronation was a far departure from those of other monarchy: he wore a bright red flannel robe topped by a white collar and covered with black speckles. He also wore a breastplate and carried a wooden scepter.

We need to be clear here: James Strang never claimed to be king of Beaver Island, or of any other patch of soil, for that matter. He claimed only to be king over his church, which he said was the true Kingdom of God that would someday spread throughout the entire world.

A brief side note: the Strangites still exist, though they are few in number, and July 8—the date of James Strang's coronation—is one of two major dates celebrated church-wide. The other . . . wait for it . . . is April 6, the day Joseph Smith established The Church of Jesus Christ of Latter-day Saints.

Once James was crowned king, things started going downhill with dizzying speed. You see, James was king over only the Strangites. They made up most of the population on the island but *not all of it.* The non-Strangites were not amused with what they considered to be a slightly off-kilter sect ruled by a seemingly unstable "king" who tried to assert his authority over everyone on the island.

Things started to get tense when the Strangites gained a complete monopoly on local government; they even managed to organize Saint James into its own county. Church members also seemed to hold a monopoly on jobs and business. Things were getting ugly.

The troubles really started when James and his followers tried to forcibly seize money and property on the island—which they determined they "deserved." The nonmembers didn't take things sitting down. Strangites were beaten up on their way to collect their mail from the post office. Some of their homes were robbed; some women and children were even seized while the men of the houses were away.

Problems reached a boiling point on July 4, 1850, when a mob of drunken fishermen vowed to kill the "Mormons" (who, of course, *weren't*) or drive them off the island. Before they could actually take any action, James Strang fired a cannon at them. You can't believe how quickly *that* brought order to an otherwise unruly crowd.

A few months after his coronation, James excommunicated George Adams, the very man who had placed the crown atop his head. We don't know what the charges were, but Adams was bitter, and he went on a campaign to discredit James. Government officials in Michigan were uneasy to begin with that some rascal up on Beaver Island had been crowned as king, and Adams's rabble-rousing was all they needed to take action. James was formally charged with treason, trespassing on government land, counterfeiting, cutting timber on federal land, theft, and a handful of other charges. He was brought to trial in Detroit, and President Millard Fillmore ordered US District Attorney George Bates to investigate the rumors about James and his group of followers. James was able to rustle up a respectable defense, and the charges against him were dropped.

He leveraged the resulting favorable press to assist him in a run as a Democrat for the 1853 Michigan House of Representatives. The voters in his district—almost all of which were members of his church, of course—gave him a sound victory. At first, the legislature tried to deny him the seat: after all, they'd heard plenty of unsavory things about him. Finally, he was allowed to speak to the body in his own defense. After two votes—the first unanimous, the second by a 49–11 margin—they allowed James to fill his seat.

His term did a great deal to reduce the prejudices against him. He introduced ten bills to the legislature, five of which passed. On February 10, 1853, the *Detroit Advertiser* said that he had conducted himself with good temper, industry, decorum, and propriety. He was reelected in 1855. His work was praised, even by his enemies.

In addition to his duties as king and his responsibilities in the legislature, James continued to be "restless," as he had been described as a young adult. He became an amateur scientist and historian. In fact, his survey of Beaver Island's natural history was published by the Smithsonian Institution and remained the definitive work on that subject for almost a century.

Meanwhile, back at the ranch, a group of people opposed to James was quietly choosing up sides and preparing for . . . well, you'll see. Some of those enemies were obvious: the people who were not members of his church continued to resent his purported power over them. But he also had some outspoken adversaries among his own people. For one, James had issued a decree that all women in the church had to wear "bloomers"—not a popular edict and one that got a lot of people riled up. Seems silly, perhaps, but you just never know.

But there was more, and it was far more serious. A Dr. H. D. McCulloch had been excommunicated—unfairly, he thought—for drunkenness and other misdeeds. Another, Thomas Bedford, had been flogged for adultery on James's orders. *Flogged.* McCulloch and Bedford joined up with non-Strangites Dr. J. Atkyn and Alexander Wentworth, who had previously been unsuccessful in an attempt to blackmail the church into paying James's bad debts.

The four managed to rustle up some pistols and made their plans while they were engaging in target practice.

Apparently James was aware that people in town were upset enough to have gotten pistols. He seemed unconcerned, telling the *Northern Islander* that he was laughing "with bitter scorn" at the threats. He refused to carry a weapon and wouldn't even *consider* hiring a bodyguard.

He shouldn't have been so cavalier.

On Monday, June 16, 1856, James was standing on the dock of the harbor at St. James when he was shot by Wentworth and Bedford. He was hit three times: one bullet grazed his head, another lodged in his cheek, and a third lodged in his spine, paralyzing him from the waist down. One of the men then savagely pistol-whipped James as he lay helpless on the ground.

The entire attack, including the pistol-whipping, took place in full view of the men aboard the *USS Michigan*, a naval vessel docked in the harbor. Several were officers. Not one person on the ship made any effort to warn James before he was shot or to help him afterward. Some accused the captain of either foreknowledge of or complicity with the murder, but those charges were never proven.

Once the pistol-whipping was finished, Wentworth and Bedford scrambled aboard the naval ship, where they both claimed sanctuary. The captain refused to give the two gunmen up to the local sheriff; instead, he took them to Mackinac Island. Talk about a joke: they were subjected to a mock trial and fined $1.25. They were then celebrated by the island residents.

Neither of the other two who plotted the murder was ever punished.

In the meantime, James—suffering from his wounds but still alive—was taken to Voree. He refused to name a successor, saying he didn't want to talk about it. The doctrine of his church required that any successor be appointed and ordained by angels. He told his apostles to await divine instruction and to take care of their families as best they could.

Then they all waited.

While James deteriorated on his deathbed back in Wisconsin, his enemies took matters into their own hands. On July 5, 1856, a mob of drunken men from Mackinac and the surrounding area descended on Beaver Island. They forcibly evicted James's estimated 2,600 followers from the island, herded them onto several steamers, robbed them of their money and other personal possessions, and callously dumped them onto the shores of Lake Michigan. Reflecting on the event, Michigan historian Byron M. Cutcheon later called it "the most disgraceful day in Michigan history."

What of the Strangites deserted on the shores of the lake? A few wandered back to Voree, where they worked to reestablish themselves. The rest scattered across the country.

And what of the Strangite church? The last of James's apostles, Lorenzo Dow Hickey, took over as its ad-hoc leader until he died in 1897; after that, Wingfield W. Watson—who had served as a high priest under James—led the church until his death in 1922. Neither Hickey nor Watson ever claimed James's office or authority. Left without a prophet to lead them, most of the Strangites (including all of James's wives) left the church in the years after James's murder; most joined the Reorganized Church of Jesus Christ of Latter Day Saints, which was officially organized in 1860. Today, as mentioned, about two hundred members of the Strangites still count themselves as members of that church.

James Strang died on July 9, 1856, at the age of forty-three, as a result of his wounds from three weeks earlier—gone, but certainly not forgotten.

Alfred and Elizabeth Ann Claridge McCune; while he waffled, she blazed new trails.

ELIZABETH ANN CLARIDGE McCUNE
TAKING ONE FOR THE SISTERS

IF YOU'VE EVER LIVED IN or around Salt Lake City, you are likely familiar with the McCune Mansion—the extravagant, red sandstone, twenty-one-room manor perched on a hill just off north Main Street. While it has served variously as a center for the arts and part of Brigham Young University over the years, it started out as a residence for a very wealthy family—and home to Elizabeth Ann Claridge McCune, who raised some of her nine children there.

It's a far cry from Nephi, Utah, where Elizabeth Ann grew up, to the affluence that built the mansion. It's an even greater leap from being *grande dame* of such a house to the humble lifestyle of a Mormon missionary in the streets of London, but those are exactly the leaps Elizabeth Ann made. And she did it all despite a husband who decided he was done with the Church—and who, some claim, lingers about today to haunt the mansion he built.

But we're getting way ahead of ourselves.

A good place to start is Hemel, Hempstead, England, where Elizabeth Ann Claridge was born on February 19, 1852. That same year, her parents—Samuel and Charlotte Joy Claridge—heeded the message of Mormon missionaries and joined the Church. The following year, 1853, the Claridge family immigrated to the United

States and joined the main body of the Saints in Zion, where they settled in the small central-Utah town of Nephi. It was in that rural setting that Elizabeth spent her childhood and where her parents raised their other eight children.

Samuel and Charlotte were hard workers, and they passed their love of industry on to their daughter. It seems Elizabeth rarely had an idle moment, spending her youthful hours sewing, knitting, crocheting, spinning yarn, and milking cows on the Claridge homestead. At the relatively tender age of fifteen, her bishop formally called her to become a telegrapher in nearby Mona, Utah. Hers was a far cry from the typical teen life today.

You can banish any images of Elizabeth dozing off between calls at the switchboard. Instead, she was busy writing her life history.[1] At *fifteen*. Most of us would think we hadn't even really *started* life at fifteen, but not Elizabeth. She lived life to its fullest and was eager to capture every detail.

In 1867, when Elizabeth was almost sixteen, her life abruptly changed when her father was called by Brigham Young to help settle Nevada's "Muddy." And *that*, my friends, was not for the faint of heart. Not even close. This wasn't one of those solo deals; it was an assignment that required Samuel Claridge to uproot his entire family from their comfy environs in Nephi and take them . . . oh, just wait.

If you're not familiar with the Muddy, listen up. A decade and a half before Samuel got his call, Mormon missionaries had established a way station at Las Vegas to serve travelers going from Utah to California. Once the Las Vegas way station was up and running, Church authorities told the missionaries to scout out potential town sites a little to the north, along the Muddy River.

Missionaries were dispatched to the area—soon to be known not-so-affectionately as simply the Muddy. And it didn't take them long to figure out why the land was still available. There were good reasons no one had settled there.

The Mormons weren't the first ones to discover the area. Spanish explorers from New Mexico were probably the first; they were looking for a way to get to California that didn't involve going through Arizona—they'd heard plenty of horror stories about the hostile Native Americans who stalked that area. (In case you don't believe things were that bad, consider Olive Oatman's experience. . . .)

The Spaniards found little but unremitting desert until they reached the area northeast of Las Vegas at the confluence of the Muddy and Virgin rivers. *This,* they thought, could be the perfect solution.

Sure enough, the place became the most popular watering hole in southern Nevada, used by early nineteenth-century trappers, traders, and government scouts. What it came right down to was this: it was a great place to visit, but you wouldn't want to live there. Why? The whole area was inundated with salts.

Then along came the Mormons. Church President Brigham Young had colonizing fever and was looking for spots to provide the necessary resources that weren't readily available in Salt Lake City. For example, he established the "iron mission" in Cedar City, Utah, to provide needed iron ore to the rest of the Mormon communities. The Muddy, he reasoned, would be a great place to grow the warm-climate crops the Saints needed and wanted. There was just one problem: that darned salt.

But what was a little salt? These were industrious, determined folk who had converted a disease-infested swamp along the Mississippi into Nauvoo, the "city beautiful." Certainly if anyone could make a go of it along the Muddy, the Mormons could.

And so the Mormons arrived in January 1865, hoes, shovels, and picks in hand. They immediately established the town of St. Thomas. A second group arrived six months later and established the town of St. Joseph nine miles to the north.

The first thing they noticed was that crops *were already* being grown along the Muddy River—crops that had been planted by the local Paiute Indians. You see, it was Paiute custom to plant wheat, corn, beans, and squash along the Muddy early in the spring. Then the Indians went north to cooler climes to hunt and gather during the heat of the summer. They returned every fall, once the worst of the heat had dissipated, to harvest whatever crops had survived the harsh summer. Needless to say, they were unhappily surprised by what they found when they returned in the fall of 1865.

The Mormons, having seen the Paiute crops already neatly planted along the river, had no problem claiming the crops (and land) for themselves, little recognizing they would be forcing the Indians into a condition of starvation. By the time fall—and harvest season—arrived along with the Paiutes, the Mormons had firmly established ownership of the land and had patiently tended the crops all summer. There was no way they were giving the crops up (or back, as was more realistically the situation).

To no one's surprise, "Indian troubles" rapidly developed. Furious about their crops being taken over by the Mormons, the Paiutes decided to "appropriate" the Mormon animals and supplies. You know, the you-take-mine-and-I'll-take-yours mentality. The Mormons were having none of it: they responded by charging the Indians with "theft" and "beggary." Before long, violence was being used to settle any disputes.

And just remember: there were wives and children, including Elizabeth, along for the ride.

Believe it or not, the Indians were only part of the problems at the Muddy. There was a reason the Paiute crops were planted in spindly little sections right along the river: the source of the Muddy was a mineral spring that rendered the soil too salty to support large-scale agriculture. The water, too, was unsuitable as a source of irrigation for large-scale crops.

The climate was also horrible for farming, as anyone who has traveled through Las Vegas in the dead of summer knows. The summer heat was searing, withering most of the crops on the stalks. There were also frequent droughts, but even in the drought-free years, Las Vegas gets only a little more than four inches of rainfall *in an entire year*. Remember, we're talking a desert.

And then there was a series of man-made disasters, undoubtedly due in part to the stress felt by settlers in a harsh, inhospitable climate. Here's just one example: on August 18, 1868, an entire town burned to the ground when two young boys lost control of the fire over which they were roasting potatoes.

While the most determined and hardy of the bunch stayed, many of the Mormon families who had been assigned to the Muddy simple pulled up stakes and left, battered by the extreme hardships they faced. Under normal circumstances, that just didn't happen—so when Brigham Young saw droves of missionaries abandoning their post, he decided he'd better check things out for himself.

In March of 1870, the prophet himself arrived at the Muddy. A quick look around convinced him that there wasn't much hope for the Muddy. That fall, an uncharacteristic flood completely wiped out a new Muddy village, West Point, resulting in more missionaries going back to the homes and farms they had left in Utah.

But the straw that broke the camel's back for the Muddy was actually a tax dispute. A new boundary survey established that the Muddy settlements were in Nevada—not Utah or Arizona. Officials in Utah, accustomed to doing things a little differently (to say the least), had always allowed people to pay their taxes in goods—you know, the random chicken, horse, or bushel of wheat. Well, the folks in Nevada didn't see it that way. They not only insisted that the missionaries at the Muddy pay back taxes, but they insisted on the taxes being paid in gold or silver.

This was a group of people who had been barely eking out an existence as it was; few of them could afford to cough up a king's ransom in gold or silver. With that, all but one family left the Muddy for good in early 1871. That final family also eventually strayed off, leaving the area abandoned. Fast-forward to today: The original Muddy Mission is somewhere at the bottom of Lake Mead, thanks to the Boulder Canyon Project that created the recreational lake.

Now you know what Elizabeth faced after quitting her job at the switchboard in Mona, saying good-bye to her childhood home and trekking to Nevada with her parents. It can't have been a dream destination for a seventeen-year-old, but reports have it that Elizabeth endured it with grace and good nature. Still possessed of an incredible work ethic, Elizabeth spent her time helping her father fashion adobe bricks so they could build a new home.

The Claridges were part of the group who left the Muddy in 1871. They returned to their home and farm in Nephi. The next year on July 1, 1872, Elizabeth Ann Claridge married her high school sweetheart, Alfred William McCune, in the Endowment House in Salt Lake City.[2]

Alfred may have spent much of his youth in Nephi, but he was actually a fairly exotic import to the area. Three years older than Elizabeth, he was born June 11, 1849, in Calcutta, India, where his British army officer father (a native of the Isle of Man) was stationed at Fort William. Alfred's mother was born in London, where her family had lived for generations. The McCunes eventually had eight children, seven sons and one daughter; Alfred was their seventh.[3] All eight children were born at Fort William, and four—three boys and their only girl—also died there. (Once in Utah, by the way, Matthew, Alfred's father, practiced plural marriage; his second and third wives bore him an additional fifteen children.[4])

The McCunes were originally members of the Plymouth Brethren Church, a Christian sect. But when they agreed to host a Church meeting in their home in 1851, they heard the tenets of The Church of Jesus Christ of Latter-day Saints—and two sailors, acting as missionaries, stayed behind after the meeting and converted the couple.[5] Alfred was only two when his family left the Plymouth Brethren and became Mormons, so he effectively spent his life in the Church. Kind of. But more about that later.

Three years after joining the Church, Matthew was transferred to Rangoon, Burma. There he spent all of his time while not at work laboring as a missionary. For the next two years, Alfred was homeschooled—by Mormon missionaries.[6]

In late 1856, Matthew resigned from the British Army, and in early December the family boarded a ship to sail from Calcutta to New York City, headed for Utah and the headquarters of the Church. Talk about a voyage—the ship didn't pull into the dock in New York until March 3, 1857. As the family set foot on land for the first time in three months, it was snowing; Alfred, who had never before seen snow, thought that salt was falling from the sky.[7] Welcome to America, kiddo.

Since they had originally set out for Utah, the McCunes stayed in New York City for only three months before boarding the train for Chicago. From there, they did what thousands before them had done: shoved all their belongings into a covered wagon and walked across the prairie to Utah, where they arrived on September 21, 1857.[8] They stayed with first one family and then another in Farmington, Utah, before moving to Nephi. And that's where Alfred met Elizabeth.

Alfred was always a hard worker, just like Elizabeth, and he tried his hand at several different things once he was old enough to work. During his middle and late teens, he worked as a farmer and stock herder,[9] a common occupation in the rural central Utah area where he lived. (You've heard it: C'mon, Mom, all the kids are doing it!) At nineteen, he left home for a time and got a job as a laborer for the Union Pacific Railroad, which was building a line through Echo Canyon in Summit County, northeast of Salt Lake City. He then worked as a cattle rancher with his brother Edward for a time. Despite dabbling on some ranches and communing with the cattle, Alfred never lost the love he developed for the railroad while helping to lay rails in Echo Canyon—and the railroad would become a major part of his life.

Alfred McCune may have begun life as a humble farmer in Nephi, but by the time all was said and done, he was one of the wealthiest men not just in Utah, but in the West. This chapter isn't about him, but it's tough to separate Elizabeth and Alfred—so suffice it to say that he had a remarkable career by any standards. The year before he and Elizabeth married, he started out by supplying hay, grain, and other provisions to workers on the Utah Southern Railroad—and by the time they had been married six years, Alfred took on two partners and built the stretch of the Utah Southern Railroad from Milford to Frisco. Next the three opened a highly profitable general store in Milford. Seems everything this guy touched turned to gold.

In 1879, McCune's joint business venture helped grade sections of the Rio Grande Railroad, Denver and South Park Railroad, Denver and New Orleans Railroad, and Oregon Short Line Railroad. In 1881, he and a partner established a six-thousand-acre cattle and horse ranch in Southern Utah. And he eventually got involved in mining, purchasing interests in a number of highly productive mines in British Columbia.

But don't think it stopped there. He also bought a one-third interest in Salt Lake City's streetcar system; under his capable leadership, the system went from mule-drawn wagons to electric-powered cars. He formed a company that took over the *Salt Lake Herald*—at the time, the *Salt Lake Tribune's* major competitor. He cofounded and became part owner of the Utah Power Company. He eventually developed railroads throughout Peru, and the company he formed there remained the largest American investor in Peru throughout the twentieth century. Yes, you could say this man was very, *very* rich.

He also got actively involved in Utah politics as the nineteenth century slid into the twentieth. He ran for the United States Senate but fell short of the necessary votes. He also ran unsuccessfully for governor of Utah, losing to seventy-year-old millionaire Simon Bamberger—the first non-Mormon, the first Democrat, and the first and only Jewish governor of Utah (he was also only the third Jew ever elected governor of any state). Ironically, Bamberger went on from a lucrative mining career to build a short-line railroad from Salt Lake City to Ogden.

So what was Elizabeth up to all this time? Well, for one thing, she was having babies—lots of them. Nine, to be exact. And any mother of even one child knows what hard work that is. But she didn't confine herself to service in her own home. An active supporter of women's rights, Elizabeth attended the 1889 International Congress of Women in London. After being voted patron of the organization, Elizabeth was entertained by Queen Victoria at Windsor Castle. Quite the honor for a farm girl from Nephi.

In 1905, she was appointed by Governor William Spray as a trustee of the Utah State Agricultural College (you'll know it as

Utah State University) in Logan. For the last two of her ten years of service at the college, she acted as vice president.[10]

She also became a sort of rock star when it came to Church service. Starting out as a counselor for the YWMIA in her ward in 1888, the next year she was called as a temple worker in the Salt Lake Temple.[11] She soon became known for her expertise in genealogical research; while Alfred was out building railroads and streetcars and power companies, Elizabeth was linking covenant generations.

In fact, Elizabeth was so devoted to genealogical research and temple work that in 1896 she traveled again to Europe—not for sightseeing, but to gather genealogical records. She went yet again in 1904, traveling with Susa Young Gates (Brigham Young's daughter) to the eastern United States, Britain, Germany, and Switzerland to see how they kept their records.

Elizabeth's subsequent Church service was substantial: in 1898 she was called to be a member of the general board of the YWMIA, in 1904 she was called to be a member of the Church's Genealogical Society, and in 1911 she was called to the Relief Society General Board.[12] In that capacity, she traveled from Canada to Mexico, preaching the gospel in stakes and missions of the Church. In essence, Elizabeth was the closest thing to a General Authority that a woman could get.

And what of Alfred? His wife may have been stacking up quite the resume of Church service, but Alfred was . . . well, he wasn't. In fact, he drifted off to such an extent that lots of people didn't think he was even a member of the Church. Clearly he was; his devout parents had him baptized at the age of eight,[13] and he married Elizabeth in the Endowment House—the equivalent of a temple. You didn't get through those doors without not only being a member, but being a member in good standing.

But it seems Alfred's quest for wealth suffocated his spiritual desires, and the status of his religious beliefs keened far enough to the other side of Mormonism that a number of people were willing to state unequivocally that he simply wasn't a Mormon. Associate Justice of the Utah Supreme Court Orlando Powers said Alfred wasn't a Mormon, a view he based on information from a number of people.[14] Mormon missionary Stuart Martin swore that Alfred wasn't a Mormon but that he had lots of Mormon friends and gave lots of money to the Church.[15] Even B. H. Roberts, LDS Church historian and member of the First Council of the Seventy, said Alfred wasn't a Mormon.[16]

We could go on all day stacking up testimonies about Alfred's lack of interest in the Mormon Church, but let's just leave it at this: his ambivalence and dearth of activity makes Elizabeth's contributions all the more amazing. Especially when you consider what would happen later.

In 1897, Alfred needed an expanded place to house his family, which now consisted of seven children—and he had plenty of money to spend on housing. After some lively negotiations with Church officials, he rented the Gardo House for the princely sum of $150 a month. It was a mansion that had served as living quarters for the President of the Church during the administrations of John Taylor and Wilford Woodruff. Located on South Temple across the street from the Beehive House, it was originally used as a place where Brigham Young could receive official callers and entertain dignitaries who had traveled considerable distances to see him. Most stick with the legend that Young borrowed the name *Gardo* from a favorite Spanish novel.[17] A few said he named it Gardo because it seemed to stand guard over the city. However it got its name, the four-story, turreted house with a tower was now home to Elizabeth Ann Claridge McCune.

The Gardo House was extravagant (not nearly what the McCunes would *eventually* live in, but that's coming up in a few minutes . . .). The exterior was stunning, but even that was eclipsed by the interior, with its spiral staircase and hand-carved, black-walnut decorative trim. It was estimated that the Church had paid as much as $50,000 just on the furnishings—and that was a *lot* of money back then.

The same year they moved into the Gardo House, Alfred decided to take his family on an extended tour of Europe, leaving the house empty for the better part of a year. And so in February

1897 they gathered up enough belongings to see them through their time abroad, where they would visit Elizabeth's homeland of England as well as France and Italy. Alfred had sightseeing on his mind. Elizabeth had something entirely different on hers.

It was a perfect opportunity to further her genealogical research, she figured, and she saw the trip as a spiritual endeavor. With that, she visited Church President Lorenzo Snow and requested a priesthood blessing before embarking on the trip. Laying his hands on her head, he suggested an additional spiritual purpose for her trip, saying, "Thy mind shall be as clear as an angel's when explaining the principles of the gospel." Those words may not have been entirely clear to Elizabeth when they were uttered, but their meaning became crystal clear as her European trip progressed.

When the McCunes left for Europe, Elizabeth was forty-five years old and had seven children. Raymond, her nineteen-year-old, was serving a full-time mission for the Church in Great Britain, and one of the things on Elizabeth's agenda was an eagerly anticipated reunion with him. (Things were apparently a bit more relaxed back then.) Elizabeth's four youngest children—Sarah Fay, seventeen; Lottie, twelve; Matthew, eight; and Elizabeth Claridge, six—accompanied their parents on the European tour.[18]

They had left behind what amounted to a mansion, but the digs they moved into at No. 4 Grange Gardens in Eastbourne—a fashionable and popular resort town—was none too shabby. Elizabeth told her close friend Susa Young Gates that the house was "large and roomy, the grounds extensive and beautiful."[19] Let's just say it was big enough that Elizabeth invited Raymond and some of the other elders in the area to stay in the house with the family. (Apparently Alfred had drifted off the Mormon grid, but one would think he couldn't have been too antagonistic against the Church if he let the missionaries move in.)

Elizabeth may have planned on doing genealogical research, but the words of President Lorenzo Snow proved prophetic almost from the time she unpacked her trunks in Eastbourne. The elders there held regular street meetings on a beachside promenade, and Elizabeth and her daughter Sarah Fay became habitual participants. They sang hymns to attract the attention of passersby, and they held the elders' hats and books while they preached to the crowds.[20] And Elizabeth also found herself playing hostess: if any in the crowd seemed interested, the elders invited them to No. 4 Grange Gardens. (You can imagine the surprise of interested onlookers when they arrived at the sumptuous dwelling . . . missionaries of any church were always known for their more-than-humble housing arrangements.)

Elizabeth's help at the street meetings eventually grew into more involvement as she accompanied the elders door to door, distributing tracts.[21] It was something that could have been terrifying for most housewives from pioneer Utah, but Elizabeth thrived on it. She realized she could withstand the occasional slammed door or disdainful glare, and found that she actually desired to play a more active role in preaching the gospel. Elizabeth "sometimes had an ardent desire to speak herself, feeling that as she was a woman she might attract more attention than the young men." Little did she know that her "ardent desire" would someday be fulfilled in the most pedestrian of ways.

It was then that Elizabeth ran into William Jarman—a genuine mouth-chomping, anti-Mormon whose sole mission in life was to attack the Church and spread scandalous rumors about Utah. By the time Elizabeth encountered him, he was a *former* member of the Church, but his status as a former member gave him credibility with the locals, who figured he must know what he was talking about. He was particularly brutal about Mormon women and their role in the family and the Church, portraying them as browbeaten objects reviled in the Mormon culture. The mission president wasn't having much luck countering his claims, since all he had were male missionaries—and who was going to believe *them*?

On October 28, 1897, the Saints from the London area assembled at Clerkenwell Town Hall for the Church's semiannual London Conference. Mission President Rulon S. Wells and his counselor, Joseph W. McMurrin, took turns addressing those present—including Elizabeth Claridge McCune and, as she remembered it, a hall bursting at the seams with "Saints and strangers" and "some very distinguished people." Extra chairs had been set up, but some still had to be turned away.

During the afternoon session, President McMurrin decided to address Jarman head-on, speaking about the falsehoods Jarman and his daughters were spreading about Mormon women being confined in ignorance and degradation. Sitting in her seat, Elizabeth thought, *Oh, if we only had one of our good woman speakers from Utah to take advantage of this grand opportunity what good it might do!*22

That thought had scarcely crossed her mind when President McMurrin pointed to her and announced, "We have with us just now, a lady from Utah who has traveled all over Europe with her husband and family, and hearing of our conference, she has met with us. We are going to ask Sister McCune to speak this evening and tell you of her experience in Utah."23 It brings to mind images of a three-ring circus.

Shocked doesn't even begin to describe how Elizabeth felt at that moment. As she put it, President McMurrin's announcement "nearly frightened me to death." As she stood on wobbly legs to begin her trip to the podium, she sent a fervent appeal to her Heavenly Father while the elders cheered her on.

Surveying her audience, she started with boldness. "I told them I had been raised in Utah and knew almost every foot of the country and most of the people. I spoke of my extensive travels in America and in Europe, and said that nowhere had I found women held in such esteem as among the Mormons of Utah," she remembered.

"Our husbands are proud of their wives and daughters; they do not consider that they were created solely to wash dishes and tend babies," she continued, "but they give them every opportunity to attend meetings and lectures and to take up everything which will educate and develop them. Our religion teaches us that the wife stands shoulder to shoulder with the husband."24

It was as though a high-voltage electric current had shot through the audience in Clerkenwell Town Hall. Elizabeth McCune, visitor from Utah and mother of seven, had done more in a few sentences to put down William Jarman than had all the elders combined. When the meeting drew to a close, she was mobbed by strangers who wanted to compliment her and ask her questions. One told her, "I have always had a desire in my heart to see a Mormon woman and to hear her speak. Madam, you carry truth in your voice and words."[25] Elizabeth couldn't help but wonder what a great work Mormon women could accomplish if only they had a place in the mission.

Sitting in the audience and undoubtedly bursting his buttons with pride was Elizabeth's missionary son, Raymond, who had been serving in the Nottingham Conference. At the conclusion of the meeting, he was transferred to London. As this incident confirms, sometimes timing is everything.

President McMurrin, watching the women who crowded eagerly around Elizabeth, made a snap decision and asked Elizabeth to accompany him to another conference the following Sunday. There she spoke along with her son Raymond on the conditions of the people in Utah. After that, every branch wanted Elizabeth McCune as a speaker, confident they could fill their halls to capacity if she was on the program.[26]

But, alas, Elizabeth's promising speaking career was cut short: it was time for the family to travel to Italy, the next stop on their agenda. In this case, though, it wasn't "out of sight, out of mind." In fact, President McMurrin thought about Elizabeth and her captivating effect on audiences so much that he wrote the men who could do something about it: the First Presidency. We need sister missionaries, he wrote. His plea was straightforward: if "a number of bright and intelligent women were called on missions to England, the results would be excellent," he penned.[27]

He wasn't alone in his opinion—nor was England the only place hankering for women to preach the gospel. At about the same time, the First Presidency received a handful of other letters from mission presidents around the world asking for sister missionaries.[28] It was obviously an idea whose time had come . . . and President Wilford Woodruff and his counselors—Joseph F. Smith and George Q. Cannon—sat up and took notice.

On March 11, 1898, after some spirited discussion, the First Presidency decided to call and set apart single sister missionaries; for the first time in Church history, these single women would be given certificates authorizing them to preach the gospel. Their decision was made public at a reception held by the Young Men and Young Women Mutual Improvement Association general boards when President George Q. Cannon announced, "It has been decided to call some of our wise and prudent women into the missionary field."[29]

We imagine the gasp that rippled through the reception that evening was similar in volume to the gasp that rippled through the Conference Center when President Thomas S. Monson announced the lowering of the missionary age.

Well, George Q. Cannon wasn't done with his announcement. Not yet. Before finishing his remarks, he spoke of the contributions of Elizabeth Ann Claridge McCune, alluding to her place in inspiring the Church to start calling sister missionaries.

At the April 1898 general conference, President Cannon announced to the Church as a whole the decision to call sister missionaries. He noted that while sister missionaries could not administer ordinances, "they can bear testimony, they can teach, they can distribute tracts, and they can do a great many things that would assist in the propagation of the gospel of the Lord Jesus Christ."[30] On April 1, 1898, Amanda Inez Knight and Lucy Jane Brimhall were set apart as the first single, certified, female proselyting missionaries in the history of the Church—in large part due to the way Elizabeth McCune spent her summer vacation.

The decision to call sister missionaries and her own role in inspiring that policy were dear to Elizabeth's heart. Later, she commented,

> While abroad I always had a burning desire in my heart to give our Father's children what I knew to be the Truth. Wherever I went to visit and had an opportunity to converse with the people I would lead up to this the uppermost topic in my

mind. Often I had the privilege of proclaiming the gospel to people who had never before heard of it. . . . I often felt if I were commissioned of God as the young men were, I could have gone into every house and entered into a quiet religious chat with the people, leaving with each one my earnest testimony.[31]

Meanwhile, back at the ranch, the McCunes had returned to Salt Lake City, and Alfred decided to build a mansion that would put anything else in the city to shame. He wanted an extravagant house that would tower impressively over the nearby streets and homes, and he made clear from the start that he would spare no expense to get exactly what he wanted.

Alfred chose architect S. C. Dallas to design the house and financed a two-year tour of America and Europe so Dallas could get inspiration. In the end, Alfred chose a Gothic revival plan with an East Asian influence—a house he and Elizabeth had seen while motoring along Riverside Drive in New York City.[32] So much for the two-year trip for the architect.

Only the best of materials were used to build the McCune mansion. The handmade tiles for the red roof came from the Netherlands; the roof alone cost more than $7,000. The exterior was fashioned of red Utah sandstone. Mahogany was shipped from San Domingo, a rare white-grained mahogany came from South Africa, and the oak came from England.

Alfred turned all the interior decorating over to Elizabeth, who had an enormous mirror transported by train from Germany; the mirror was so big it had to be carried in a custom-made railroad car. The fireplaces were built of exotic stone such as onyx and Nubian marble from Egypt, and the walls were embellished with silk tapestries and Russian leather. The house was finished in 1901 at a cost of more than a million dollars; for many years it was considered the costliest home in Salt Lake City and one of the grandest in the entire western United States. (In 1974, it was listed on the National Register of Historic Places.[33])

Alfred's involvement in his various business concerns continued, as did his almost insatiable drive to accumulate wealth—both of which came at a dear price for Elizabeth, who found that Alfred distanced himself from the Church even farther. Though she was devastated by that, she remained a loyal companion to him. Privately, she prayed continually that he would eventually discover a resurgence of his faith.

On that account, she would be sorely disappointed.

Alfred's long-time friend, Heber J. Grant—yes, *that* Heber J. Grant—opined that by 1908, Alfred's desire to earn money had simply overwhelmed his Mormon faith.[34] That's not all, Heber said—he felt that Alfred's pursuit of wealth had also influenced the loss of faith among the McCune children. And, of course, Elizabeth spent much of her time alone as Alfred continued to pursue his business interests.

As for Elizabeth, she had a much more spiritual attitude toward the couple's wealth. She saw it as a stewardship and spent her efforts making sure that the family supported those in need and made generous donations to the Church. In her later life, she also used their position of wealth in her Church callings.

In 1920, Alfred and Elizabeth decided to move to California; Alfred's health was deteriorating, and doctors felt the warm climate would be beneficial for him. Remember the incredible mansion they built? On October 7, 1920, they donated it to the LDS Church—so it would seem that Alfred was simply disinterested but not antagonistic toward the Church. The Church immediately converted the million-dollar home into the LDS School of Music. It has undergone a few transitions since then; it was the Brigham Young University Salt Lake City Center until 1972, then the Virginia Tanner Modern Dance School, and is now privately owned and used for wedding receptions and other events. One of the smokestacks was toppled during Salt Lake City's tornado in August 1999, but that has since been restored.

Back to the McCunes: Albert was seventy-one when they moved to Los Angeles; the pair moved into the Hotel Van Nuys for three months before buying a home on Kingsley Drive for $30,000.

During the next few years, Elizabeth's health also started to decline. In 1923, they sold their California home and returned to Salt Lake, when they started construction on a new home—much more modest this time—in the northeast part of the city. In spring of 1924, while the house was still under construction, the couple went on an extended vacation to Bermuda. You know, to escape all the construction debris.

While they were in Bermuda, Elizabeth took a real turn for the worse, and they rushed back to Salt Lake, taking up residence in the Hotel Utah. Her health worsened rapidly, and her large, extended family rushed to the city to be by her side. Elizabeth Ann Claridge McCune died in Salt Lake City on August 1, 1924.

A public funeral was held for her at Temple Square. She was buried in Nephi.

Two years later—in November 1926—Alfred went with some other family members on a vacation to Europe. These last couple of trips turned out to be bad omens for the McCunes, though: Alfred never returned to the United States, dying on March 28, 1927, in Cannes, France. But, as they say, all eventually come home again—and Alfred was buried next to Elizabeth in Nephi.

That may not be the end of the McCunes—or, at least, of Alfred.

In 1990, the people who bought the mansion found that after eighty years of wear and tear, it was looking a bit shabby. Maybe even a bit spooky. And it had to qualify as one of the most expensive fixer-uppers ever on the market. No matter; Phil McCarthey and his family committed to giving the home the tender loving care it deserved, and they worked to restore it to its former glory.

Soon after that restoration was complete, the McCarthey family hosted a Christmas party for extended family in the mansion—the first time since 1919 that the home had been used for a family Christmas celebration. Well, someone or something seemed delighted at the celebration: the lights of the ballroom kept popping on, despite Phil's attempts to keep them under control. He finally conceded defeat.[35]

Since then, a curious, gentle, ghostly man in a black cape continues to appear to visitors—but only when a visitor is alone in a room. One of Phil McCarthey's sons told him that a calm, non-threatening man dressed in a black cape appeared, watched him for a time, and then disappeared.

Could that man in the cape be Alfred McCune?

Maybe. But he's not the only one in the mansion.

A little girl who strongly resembles the child in a portrait that still hangs in the mansion has been seen walking in and out of the mirror that hangs on the west wall of the first floor. According to reports, her footprints have been found in several rooms; they always both start and end in the middle of the floor. She loves to attend the weddings and receptions that are held in the mansion, and she has been caught on film on more than a few occasions.

Like any creative little girl, she plays with and reorganizes things in unique ways—especially things that were already prearranged professionally for weddings and receptions planned for the next day.

Apparently, though, the man in the black cape and the girl in the gown are not the only spooky things that have gone on in the mansion. Soon after the music school opened in the mansion, organ music was heard loud and clear when no one was in the house. People have also heard voices and felt cold spots throughout the mansion. Lights go on and off without being operated, and doors open and close at will. Doors that were locked are found unlocked. And unlocked doors are found locked—even when there is no locking mechanism.

In fact, the McCune Mansion is one of the most popular stops on the "Haunted Houses" tours conducted each fall in Salt Lake.

Could that be due to Alfred McCune? You just never know . . .

Martin Harris—years past the time he was supposedly murdered by disgruntled Mormons.

MARTIN HARRIS
"REPORTS OF MY DEATH HAVE BEEN GREATLY EXAGGERATED"

HEY, WAIT—THAT "REPORTS OF MY death" quote belonged to Mark Twain, not Martin Harris.

But as you're about to find out, it might as well have been penned by Harris himself.

In Twain's case, he—real name, Samuel Clemens—was on a round-the-world speaking tour he'd started in 1895. Fast on the heels of some unsuccessful investments and publishing ventures, he was hoping to garner enough money in speaking engagements to pay off the "considerable debt" he'd left behind in America.

While he was in London, someone started a wild rumor that Twain was gravely ill. In actuality, as Twain would later clarify, it was his *cousin*, James Ross Clemens, who was hovering at death's door—not him. Happily, the cousin beat the odds and recovered.

But things didn't stop there—not even close. Next came the rumor that Twain was dead. A couple of enterprising newspapers even printed his obituary. When an intrepid reporter finally caught up with Twain and wired him for his reaction, he wired back the now-famous line: "The reports of my death have been greatly exaggerated."

Enter Martin Harris.

You probably already know a lot about him—you know, losing the 116 pages, mortgaging the farm to pay for printing the Book of Mormon, witnessing the angel and the plates, showing the hieroglyphics to an Egyptian scholar, and leaving the Church, for starters. What you might *not* know is that fifty-four years before Mark Twain's adventure, Martin Harris also found his own cold, dead body being tossed about by the rumor mills.

In late June 1841, the following notice started appearing in newspapers *all over the United States*:

> Martin Harris, who was one of the witnesses to the book of Mormon, and who has been for some time lecturing in Illinois against the Mormons, was found dead last week, having been shot through the head. He was, no doubt, murdered.[1]

Historian Ardis E. Parshall thinks the notice might have first appeared in New York's *Journal of Commerce*—but regardless of its start, the story spread like wildfire. The article and accompanying obituary in the Rochester *Democrat*, which seized the opportunity for a glowing eulogy, were especially lengthy. Some credited the news to "a letter written somewhere in the neighborhood of Nauvoo, the Mormon city."

Regardless of its nebulous start, subsequent reports wasted no time in blaming the "murder" on the Mormons of that fair city. A report in a Philadelphia paper had this to say about the alleged death:

> Martin Harris, one of the earliest of the Mormon sect, has recently been murdered by these fanatics. He had recently abandoned them and was exposing their wickedness in Illinois, when he fell a victim to their ferocity.

But that wasn't all. An editor in western New York who had personally known Harris wrote what could only be called a colorful obituary about the man—an obituary that was eagerly snapped up by many other papers. In it we learn that, while "illiterate and naturally of a superstitious turn of mind," Harris was at least an honest man and not as "destitute of character and intelligence" as the Prophet Joseph Smith and those who followed him. In fact, stated the obituary, Harris was simply "deluded" when it came to Mormonism and never wished "to delude others knowingly."

As a result of Harris's association with Mormonism, the obituary stated, "He was subjected to many scoffs and rebukes, all of which he endured with a meekness becoming a better cause." And since most of the early Saints were "destitute," it claimed, "Mr. Harris was the only man of wealth among the early Mormons, and many were the calls made upon his purse for the purpose of feeding Smith and fostering his humbug in its incipient stages."

Saying Harris was eventually "fleeced of his goodly estate," the obituary continued by saying he had gone to Missouri:

> We have not seen him since, and supposed until we saw the announcement of his death, and the cause of it conjectured, that he was still among the most zealous and conspicuous of Jo Smith's followers. But we were wrong. . . . He had been so long a confidant of Smith and his leading associates, and had seen so much of their villainy that he undoubtedly felt it a duty to expose them and their debasing doctrines. —Hence his lectures against Mormonism in Illinois, and hence, too, his probable murder by some of that sect.

The obituary concluded with a statement that Harris was about fifty-five years of age. After specifying that his first wife had died in Palmyra after refusing to accompany Harris to "the Promised Land," the article said he had returned to Wayne County, Ohio, and married again.

You've heard the joke about knowing it's a rough day when you see your own obituary in the news? Just imagine how Harris (and, for that matter, Mark Twain) must have felt.

Well, the good folks in Kirtland knew for a fact that Harris wasn't dead at all, and Ohio's *Painesville Telegraph* quickly tried to set the record straight. After agreeing with all the printed eulogies about his outstanding character, the paper reported, "Martin Harris is a living witness of what shall be said of him after his death." Because, the article continued, "He is now, or was two days since, alive and well, at his residence in Kirtland."

Undoubtedly red in the face, the editor in Pennsylvania published a brief retraction of the murder story, reporting that the *Painseville Telegraph* in Ohio "says that Martin Harris the Mormon has not been found dead any where, but is alive and hearty, at his residence in Kirtland." Subsequent retractions, when they eventually came, were equally brief. Embarrassment can do that to a person.

Back in the day, of course, news tended to spread a bit more slowly than we're accustomed to; no hasty corrections on the evening news or retractions gone viral on the Internet. As a result, the story of Harris's death, along with his sensational obituary, continued to make the rounds throughout the country well into the middle of July. In fact, a newspaper in Hartford, Connecticut, reported on July 10 that Harris had been "found dead, having been shot through the head with a pistol. No doubt was entertained of his having been murdered."

Sometime toward the end of July, after nearly a month, the stories finally died down. Martin Harris, and everyone else for that matter, went back to life as usual.

Martin Harris *did* part ways with the Church—but that's a story for another day. Though it seemed he had some struggles with Joseph Smith, he never retracted his testimony of the authenticity of the plates from which the Prophet translated the Book of Mormon. Nor did he ever deny seeing the angel who showed him those plates.

And all's well that ends well, as you might say: after more than thirty years away from the Church, Harris made his way in 1870 to Cache County, Utah. Once a wealthy landowner, he was by that time destitute. Members of the Church in Ohio donated a total of two hundred dollars to him, pitching in to help him make the trip to Utah. There, he spent the last four and a half years of his life living with relatives in Cache County. There he was rebaptized. And there he died (but more about that in a minute).

In 1871, he gave the following testimony, which was eventually reported in the *Latter Day Saints' Herald* on October 15, 1875, three months after his death:

> [No] man ever heard me in any way deny the truth of the Book of Mormon, the administration of the angel that showed me the plates; nor the organization of the Church of Jesus Christ of Latter Day Saints, under the administration of Joseph Smith Jun., the prophet whom the Lord raised up for that purpose, in these latter days, that he may show forth his power and glory. The Lord has shown me these things by his Spirit—by the administration of holy angels. . . .

So, just in case you've heard rumors to the contrary, there you have it, straight from the horse's mouth. And as this whole story shows, rumors are never a great source of information.

In the end, much like Mark Twain, Martin Harris outlived all those "exaggerated" reports of his death. In fact, he managed to live until 1875, when he died in Clarkston, Utah, at the ripe old age of ninety-two.

Oh, and he died of old age. No pistols, bullets, or ferocious Mormons involved.

Sons and daughters of George A. Smith. In front, sitting: Pearl Smith. Seated, left to right: Clarissa Smith Williams, Bathsheba Smith Merrill, John Henry Smith, Sarah Maria Smith Colton, Mary Amelia Smith Wimmer. Standing, left to right: Elizabeth Smith Cartwright, Margaret Smith Parry, Charles Warren Smith, Grace Libby Smith Cheever, and Priscilla Smith Taylor.

CLARISSA SMITH WILLIAMS
A CHICKEN IN EVERY POT,
A MATERNITY CHEST IN EVERY WARD

FEW WOMEN IN THE WARD are busier than the Relief Society president; after all, she's sort of the female equivalent of the bishop. There's compassionate service to render, food orders to fill out, visiting teaching to coordinate, and a whole lot of women to look after. Whatever's going on in the ward—and sometimes that's a *lot*—the Relief Society president is on top of it.

And if you think *that's* a big job, consider this: almost a century ago, the ward Relief Society president was *also* expected to keep on hand a fully stocked and replenished "maternity chest," ready at a second's notice to be loaned out should any sister in her ward be ready to deliver a bundle of joy. Kind of like the one-stop shop for turning your bedroom into a labor and delivery room.

That was all thanks to Clarissa Smith Williams, the sixth general president of the Relief Society and the first native Utahan to serve in that post. She was at the helm of the organization from 1921 until 1928. And, as you'll see, she was a visionary when it came to health care—especially maternal health care—and a range of related social issues.

Let's flash back sixty-two years from the time she was called as president to see what led up to the mantra of a maternity chest in every ward. (Where did they keep it, anyway? In the ward library?)

Clarissa Smith was born April 21, 1859, the first of five daughters born to Apostle George A. Smith and his seventh and last wife, Susan Elizabeth West Smith. Clarissa, like almost every other baby of the day, was born at home—but hers wasn't any ordinary home. Her parents lived in the residential wing of the Church Historian's Office in Salt Lake City, and that's where she made her entrance into the world.

And here's a potentially colorful note: her parents shared the apartment with the Apostle's first wife, Bathsheba W. Smith, and her children. As it turns out, though, all the color was pleasant, as the two wives and their children lived very harmoniously in what was for the day some exceptionally comfortable digs. (After all, plenty of folks were still pitching tents and living in log cabins, with covered wagons pulling in to the city on a regular basis.)

From all accounts, it seems that Clarissa had a happy childhood. She certainly moved among the upper class. Her best friends were the daughters of President Brigham Young, who lived just around the corner.[1] It may have been a sign of things to come, but Clarissa started her Relief Society service early in life when she was called to be a visiting teacher at the tender young age of sixteen.[2] Clarissa's parents saw to it that she and her sisters received the best education available at the time in the Utah Territory. In 1975, she received a teaching certificate from the Normal Department of the University of Deseret (later to become the University of Utah).[3] Certificate in hand, she opened her own private school in Parowan, Utah, for a time.

On July 17, 1877, Clarissa married William Newjent Williams, her sweetheart of two years. It was the shortest honeymoon in history: the very next day he left on a mission to his native land of Wales. While he was knocking doors and holding street meetings in Wales, she was teaching school in Parowan, counting down the days until his return.

William turned out to be a good catch. He went on to become a state senator, a regent at the University of Utah, and a successful businessman. And this was a guy with his priorities straight: even with all he had to occupy his time, his family was always his main concern.[4] Theirs was a large family. He and Clarissa went on to have eleven children—three of whom died before reaching adulthood—and lived to celebrate their fiftieth wedding anniversary.

Clarissa was also busy (as if having *eleven children* wasn't enough!). While she was busy having babies, she served as secretary and president of the Relief Society in both the Salt Lake Seventeenth Ward and Salt Lake Stake.[5] Lucky for her, William was a major support in those endeavors. Later in her life, she wrote:

> After I was married and had seven children, I was asked to be secretary of the Seventeenth Ward Relief Society. I felt that I could not do this with all my little babies. But my husband said, "My dear, you must do it; it is the very thing you need; you need to get away from the babies, and I will help you all I can, either by taking care of the children or making out your reports or copying your minutes, or any other thing I can do."[6]

That's the spirit, William! Time out for mom. . . .

Good thing William felt that way, because Clarissa's responsibilities in the Relief Society got exponentially greater. In 1901, the fourth Relief Society general president asked Clarissa to serve as treasurer of the Relief Society and as a member of its general board. That president was none other than Bathsheba W. Smith, Clarissa's father's first wife—the one who shared the apartment in which Clarissa grew up. You have to say this for them: they certainly knew each other well.

Ten years later, in 1911, Clarissa became first counselor to Emmeline B. Wells, the fifth general president of the Relief Society. When Wells died eleven years later, in 1921, President Heber J. Grant called Clarissa Smith Williams to be sixth general president of the Relief Society and the editor of the *Relief Society Magazine*. (It was under Clarissa, incidentally, that visiting teaching messages were first published in the magazine—sort of like we enjoy today in the *Ensign*.)

By then, responding in great part to national conditions generally, Clarissa Smith Williams had an agenda, and with her new calling, she was in a position to carry out that agenda in a dramatic way.

For one thing, it was an exciting time for women in America. They had just been given the right to vote—something we totally take for granted—and there was a general air of eager anticipation as women considered how they might be able to make a difference in the places where they lived. Clarissa was solidly in the curve as she wrote, "We have been given such blessings as have never been given to women in any other age, and we should in every way endeavor to live up to them."[7]

Opportunities for women had been a theme of Clarissa's service in the general Relief Society presidency. She had been one of nine delegates to the International Council of Women in Rome, Italy, in May 1914. During World War I, she had served as chairwoman of the Utah Women's Committee of the National Council of Defense. She continued that emphasis during her time as president, serving as a member of the National Council of Women.

But Clarissa's passion—and, as a result, the crowning achievement of her time as president—focused on social problems, particularly those involving mothers and children. She spearheaded the organization of the first Relief Society Social Service Department with a jam-packed agenda that would have sent even the most organized executive over the edge. Under Clarissa's supervision, the department distributed free milk to infants, operated summer camps for underprivileged children, funded loans for training public health nurses, provided free health exams for preschool children, helped needy girls and women find jobs, held health clinics, placed children for adoption, sent aid to war-torn Europe, operated a storehouse that distributed goods to the poor, and offered training courses on child rearing, disease, care for the sick, hygiene, crime prevention, relief work, and other kinds of topics.[8]

Whew.

And as if that wasn't enough, in 1924, under her supervision, the Relief Society established the Cottonwood Maternity Hospital, which remained in operation until 1963.⁹ The hospital, located at 404 East 5600 South in Salt Lake, was for decades a major facility in childbirth care that was maintained by the Cottonwood Stake Relief Society under the direction of the general Relief Society presidency.

And you thought thinning sugar beets once a year was a tough assignment.

Back in the day, Cottonwood was considered a region "out in the boondocks" whose residents didn't have easy access to medical care. When two different mothers in the neighborhood died during childbirth from conditions that could have been prevented if they had received proper care, Clarissa swung into action: out-of-town places needed "to establish maternity hospitals where possible,"¹⁰ she said, and Cottonwood was first on her list. Marshalling the stake Relief Society, Clarissa launched her plan.

First off, they needed a building. After poking all over Cottonwood, they settled on a spacious two-story brick home on one and a half acres owned by Neil McMillan; the family had lost a son in the war and wanted a change of scenery. Expansive brick additions were eventually built on the back to accommodate twenty-three patient rooms, which had initially been on the second floor of the house. By the time the hospital was in full operating mode, the office, reception area, laboratory, birthing room, and labor room were on the original first floor of the house. The basement housed the laundry, kitchen, heating equipment, and water softening equipment. And the original second floor served as living quarters for the nurses.¹¹

Yes, you read that right. The nurses lived up top. That's what we call never being able to get away from your work.

The hospital was opened in October 1924. Considered a Church facility, it was dedicated on December 10 that same year by Elder Melvin J. Ballard of the Council of the Twelve.

Expenses were kept as low as possible so every woman who needed it and wanted to could afford to use the hospital. And we're talking low: in 1949, after twenty-five years of operation, the hospital raked in a net profit of thirty-five cents.[12] Much of the labor associated with the hospital was simply donated, and for several years each woman in the stake was asked to donate one quart of home-bottled fruit to the place. Once the hospital got on a bit more even financial keel, fruit was purchased and Relief Society sisters bottled it in the hospital kitchen. Donating their labor, of course.

At first, the delivery bed was located on the main floor of the house. After delivering her baby, each woman was carried upstairs (oh, give me *that* job!), where she spent two weeks in one of ten beds on the second floor. The nursery was a small room that had previously been a nook in the McMillan home. Cost for the two weeks was forty dollars, which covered "everything including operating table, all medicine (except doctor's prescriptions), and use and laundering of the babies' layettes."[13]

In the first ten months of the hospital's operation, 110 babies were born there.

As she moved into her tenure as general Relief Society president, Clarissa had been especially concerned about infant and mother mortality rates. They weren't the best; in fact, they were abysmal. The Church vital records for 1922 show that 58 mothers and 751 babies died that year in childbirth.[14] If Clarissa had been able to see into the future of her hospital in Cottonwood, she would have undoubtedly been very pleased: not a single mother lost her life during the first twenty-six years of operation, according to a *Deseret News* article marking that milestone, despite the fact that thousands of babies had been born there.[15]

Back to Clarissa: she remained concerned about mothers and their babies, and she had an ingenious idea on how to fund the programs she planned. And if you've ever wondered why the Relief Society emblem is festooned with stalks of wheat, you're about to find out.

You see, the Church—or, more accurately, the Relief Society—had a "wheat fund." It actually started sometime in the 1860s, when the men of the Church started growing wheat and donating it to the Church as an income-producing venture. Well, the men tried for years to make the project work, but they, according to Daniel H. Wells, "have continued to let the grain go." It was time, Brigham Young agreed, to "see if the sisters will be more successful."[16]

And so it was that in 1876, Brigham Young asked Emmeline B. Wells—Daniel's wife and later to become the fifth general president of the Relief Society—to organize a wheat storage program. It was to be squarely in the court of the women: while husbands were supposed to help and support their wives, the women were to do the work. As President John Taylor put it, "We brethren . . . should assist our 'female brethren' in the work."

The sisters took on the task with aplomb. In fact, Sarah Kimball stood up and stated, "We have the faith, nerve, and land to build upon." The land was probably the least of the problem; the faith and nerve were probably the distinguishing factors.

So the women went to work, initially gleaning wheat from existing fields. As they sold their wheat as well as collected money from their sisters, they were eventually able to buy their own land and even build their own granaries. They began watching the market like hawks, buying up as much wheat as they could while the prices were low.

Imagine, if you will, the discussions at Relief Society meetings in those days. They centered around how to combat weevil and when to buy and sell, among other agriculture-related subjects.

As the program continued, the men required occasional reminders of exactly *whose* project this was. After all, in the early 1900s it was unusual for women to be in charge of anything outside the walls of their own homes (and sometimes not even there). At one point, the First Presidency distributed a letter to bishops informing them that they had no rights when it came to wheat matters—those were solely in the hands of the Relief Society.

Apparently they had conveniently forgotten that directive when the US government came to the brethren asking for help for European countries that had been devastated during World War I. The brethren offered the wheat without first asking the women.

They were rapidly made to recognize their mistake. And apologize. And make amends.

The wheat program was no fly-by-night affair; it lasted for just more than a hundred years. In 1978, when all Church departments were correlated, the money from the wheat fund was incorporated into the general Church welfare fund. At that time, Relief Society general president Barbara B. Smith turned over 226,291 bushels of Relief Society wheat—worth more than $1.6 million—as well as additional assets worth three-quarters of a million dollars.

During its hundred-year history, the wheat fund had been used to care for the poor and needy. The Relief Society also donated wheat to ease the burdens of survivors of the 1906 San Francisco earthquake, World War I, and World War II.

And, as you've probably guessed by now, it was used by Clarissa Smith Williams—after getting the support of her general board—"in the interest of maternity and motherhood throughout the Church."[17]

And so it was. The Church used the funds to train nurses' aides and provide scholarships to upper-division nursing students. Stakes and wards used the funds for everything from opening maternity hospitals to assembling maternity loan chests (if you don't know what those are, don't panic; we'll explain in a minute). In the third year of Clarissa's administration, 1924, the Presiding Bishopric reported that the lives of five hundred children had been saved just that year by the efforts of the Relief Society.

Probably the most colorful part of this whole story were the maternity chests and bundles that Clarissa's general board prescribed in 1923 for every ward—using the interest from the wheat fund.[18]

Simply put, each ward was to have a maternity chest as part of its supplies. You know, hymn books, gospel art, lesson manuals, and maternity chests. The chests were to hold everything needed to safely deliver a baby and to subsequently dress that baby. The philosophy was that articles in the chest could be sold, rented, loaned, or given to the needy—and replaced and replenished after use so the ward always had a full chest on standby.

Whenever possible, a nurse was to assist in putting together the maternity chests and bundles. Depending on the situation, a stake might be the one to house the chest. In her missive announcing the program, Clarissa specified that "the work might be undertaken as a stake, with the wards pooling their funds in the stake board." As an example, she pointed out, "The Pioneer Stake in Salt Lake City operates a large loan cupboard or chest for the whole stake, under the direction of the stake board."[19]

And to think we store music for the ward choir in our cupboard . . .

Clarissa also spared no words in detailing how the chests were to be cared for. They were, she wrote, to "be kept absolutely clean and sanitary." She suggested that Relief Societies consult with local doctors or nurses on the proper sterilization and care of the things in the chest. If a hospital is nearby, she suggested, workers should sterilize the materials in the chest using hospital facilities.

And here's a great one. If sanitary pads for use immediately following birth couldn't be purchased, Clarissa wrote, cloth could be used—but only if baked for at least an hour or, if needed the same day, ironed thoroughly with a hot iron.

Oh, the things we really *do* take for granted.

As a final piece of instruction, Clarissa admitted that some wards or stakes wouldn't be able to put together a complete chest at the drop of a hat. In those cases, she specified, they should start with whatever they could and then gradually add the other supplies.

Ready for it? Take a look at what the Relief Societies had to put together for the maternity chests, which were used in the large number of home births during that period. This list is not only daunting but gives a great look at what was involved in childbirth during the 1920s:

MATERNITY CHEST
1 bedpan
2 hot water bags
1 ice bag

1 enema can (all attachments: nose, rectal, douche points, rubber
    tubing, clamps)
1 catheter—rubber and glass
1 rectal tube
1 pitcher—1-quart size
1 slop bucket
1 electric pad

Surgical Supplies
Absorbent cotton
Bandages and gauze
Boracic acid
Lysol
Argyrol tablets, 1-grain
Glycerine
Olive oil
Vaseline tubes
Iodine
Umbilical cord tie
Medicine droppers—1/2 dozen
Measuring glasses—1/2 dozen
Soap—toilet and laundry
Witch hazel
Applicators (toothpicks wrapped with cotton)
Thermometers

Emergency Supplies
All types of infants' apparel—used, repaired, and new
Mother's apparel—underwear and gowns

Bedding
Pillowcases
Sheets
Spreads
Towels, washcloths
Tray covers
Quilts, blankets, etc.

MATERNITY BUNDLES

I

1 yard white oilcloth
3 sanitary packs (to be used after birth)
Safety pins
Olive oil
Talcum powder
Boracic acid, prepared solution
Lysol
Medicated cotton
Gauze
1 bar soap

II

1 yard white oilcloth
1 white sheet
1 pad, 1-yard square
1 gown
2 large perineal pads
12 large sponges
1 binder for breast, with pins
1 binder for abdomen, with pins
1 pair long hip stockings, made of outing flannel, supplied with
    safety pins
6 towels
1 pair rubber gloves
1 receiving blanket
1 cord tie and cord dressing
1 baby band
4 sponges
1 diaper
Piece of absorbent cotton

FIRST BABY NECESSITIES:
Shirt, band, gown, diaper, blanket
LAYETTE: 6 dresses, 4 skirts, 3 shirts, 3 strips flannel, 3 dozen
    diapers, 4 nightgowns, 1 blanket

<u>Note</u>: Baby clothes should be simple and comfortable and not longer than 24 inches

And there you have it. Just a bit of social commentary on this exhaustive list: note that underwear and gowns for the mother are listed under "Emergency Supplies." Yup, we'd say a mother with no gown or underwear just might constitute an emergency, all right. And note that the second, more complete maternity bundle contains sixteen sponges but only one diaper. We guess you could, in a pinch, use some of those sponges as diapers . . .

While you're at it, survey that list of layette supplies: 4 *skirts* for the newborn baby? Well, best to be prepared in case they were on their way to church meetings when interrupted by the onset of labor and delivery.

And a *slop bucket*? Face it: indoor plumbing with the associated accoutrements didn't become standard in households in the American West until a decade or two earlier . . . and it didn't reach rural areas until sometime in the 1830s.

Oh, dear.

In all seriousness, it's virtually impossible to calculate the dramatic effect Clarissa Smith Williams had on the health of mothers and babies in the Church. Many of us had grandmas who undoubtedly benefitted from her devotion.

She'd made a tremendous difference during her tenure as president, but she asked to be released from her calling in October 1928 due to failing health. She was succeeded in that position by Louise Y. Robison.

Less than eighteen months later, the woman who had saved so many lives died of nephritis on March 8, 1920, in her home in Salt Lake City. She was buried in the Salt Lake City Cemetery.

Olive Ann Oatman, sporting the blue cactus chin tattoo she was given by the Mohave Indians.

OLIVE ANN OATMAN
THE GIRL WITH THE BLUE TATTOO

WHAT'S A NICE MORMON GIRL like Olive Ann Oatman doing living with a tribe of bloodthirsty Apaches? The story of how she got there is radically colorful all on its own—and it scarcely holds a candle to what happened to her after that.

But let's not get ahead of ourselves. In fact, let's start at the very beginning, when no one in Olive's family was even *thinking* about Indians.

The Oatmans—Roys (rhymes with "voice") and his wife, Mary Ann Sperry—were your average, peaceful, run-of-the-mill farmers in La Harpe, Hancock County, Illinois, where Olive Ann was born on September 7, 1837. She was the second of what would become the Oatmans' seven children.

Then along came the Mormons. In 1839, as Olive was turning two, Roys and Mary Ann gave up their Methodist faith and joined The Church of Jesus Christ of Latter-day Saints, pledging their allegiance to the Prophet Joseph Smith. From that time on, they were your average, peaceful, run-of-the-mill *Mormon* farmers in rural Illinois. They were doggedly true to the faith.

But all that changed in 1844, when the Prophet was martyred. Olive was seven. Her parents had been ardent supporters of Joseph Smith, but they stridently rejected the leadership of Brigham

Young. In all fairness, they were not alone; as you'll remember, there was quite a bit of uproar as the young Church tried to figure out what to do next. After all, it was the first time they'd faced this particular dilemma. Instead of aligning with Brigham Young, the Oatmans fell under the spell of a persuasive visionary and self-designated "seer and revelator" named James Colin Brewster.

Before going on with Olive's story, it's important that we say a word or two about Brewster so you'll have a clear idea of what was happening. You see, Brewster wasn't exactly a newcomer on the scene. His parents had converted to Mormonism when he was a young child. In 1836, when he was ten, Brewster claimed he had been visited by the angel Moroni—yes, *that* angel Moroni. And that wasn't all—Brewster made continuing claims to divine revelation, which the Prophet on occasion referred to as "phony." Within a year, at the age of eleven, Brewster claimed to be a prophet. When he refused to back down and continued to claim divine revelations, he was disfellowshipped from the Church. At the age of *eleven*. (He never changed his story either. In the 1850 US Census for Socorro, New Mexico Territory, he listed his occupation as "Mormon Prophet.")

By 1842, he had written a book in which he claimed that the lost book of Esdras had been revealed anew "by the gift of God" in the "last days." Revealed to him, of course. Everyone in Nauvoo and surrounding areas knew he was not on solid footing with the Church. Most people tolerated him but didn't pay him much attention, though he did attract a handful of followers.

But in 1844, when the Prophet was martyred, Brewster stepped up his game. With Joseph Smith out of the way, Brewster got aggressive. He based his group in Springfield, Illinois, and targeted Mormons who were feeling a little lost as they searched for a new prophet-leader.

In 1848, he and Hazen Aldrich came up with their own solution when they founded the Church of Christ. Forget squabbling over a mere leader—this was the *organization* they claimed was the rightful and true successor to the Mormon Church. Aldrich was chosen as president; Brewster was one of his two counselors in the First Presidency. The other was fellow apostate Jackson Goodale.

And now a brief note about Aldrich, himself a pretty colorful character. He was baptized a Mormon in 1832 by Orson Pratt and entered the waters of baptism literally alongside future Apostle Amasa M. Lyman. Ordained an elder and then a high priest, two years later he participated in the Zion's Camp expedition to Missouri, widely considered a training ground for future Church leaders. In 1836, he was the first missionary to preach in the area now known as Quebec. Then, suddenly, he apostatized in Kirtland, Ohio, in 1837. First he joined up with the church founded by James Strang; almost immediately, he was excommunicated for incest. Next he joined the Church of Christ, which had been organized by David Whitmer. That organization simply petered out within a few months, so Aldrich was footloose and fancy-free, looking for another church to join when Brewster came along.

The two founded their church and actively started soliciting followers. Enter the Oatmans, who, as we pointed out, were disenchanted with Brigham Young. Still considering themselves Mormons, the Oatmans nevertheless took up with Brewster and Aldrich—not exactly a match made in heaven.

Unless you've been living under a rock, you know what happened to the Saints in Nauvoo after Joseph Smith was martyred. While everyone else packed up their dolls and dishes and headed for the Rocky Mountains, Brewster was busy receiving revelation for his followers—and he soundly rejected the Rockies as their settling place. Instead, he declared that the promised land—for *his* Saints, at least—was a place he called "the Land of Bashan," situated at the confluence of the Gila and Colorado Rivers on the present-day border between Arizona and California. He touted it as a "blissful land of overflowing richness" and assured his followers that the Indians who inhabited the land were strictly men of peace, with no disposition to ever go to war.

As it turned out, *that* couldn't have been more wrong—the peaceful Indians part, we mean. But again, we're getting ahead of ourselves. . . .

By this time, Aldrich had started to doubt Brewster's prophetic abilities. So when Brewster and Goodale rounded up their followers to set out for the Land of Bashan, Aldrich himself cut ties and returned to Kirtland.

And so it was that Brewster's followers pulled out of Independence, Missouri, on August 9, 1850. They numbered about eighty-five pioneers (some sources say as many as ninety-three) in twenty wagons—among them the Oatman family: forty-three-year-old Roys; his pregnant wife, Mary Ann; and their seven children, including an infant son.

There you have it: while Brigham Young's followers were still making their way to Salt Lake City—by now a thriving city—Brewster and *his* followers veered to the south. Instead of finding their way along a well-worn trail peppered with forts and supply stations, the Oatmans and company were blazing new paths across treacherous and uninhabitable stretches of desert in hostile Indian territory (despite Brewster's "vision" of the Indians in that area as men of peace).

Before long, things weren't going well. Frequent disagreements erupted between Brewster and Goodale. And they weren't the only offenders: there were lots of spats (and some outright fist fights) between other members of the pioneer band as well. Apparently, tempers were short all over the place. Still, they trudged on—until shortly after they crossed into present-day New Mexico, that is. At that point, Brewster abruptly sat down on the ground and announced that he was "as close to heaven" as he intended to go. He set up a colony near Socorro Peak and planted his roots. (Years later, Brewster drifted toward California, preaching spiritualism along the way; at some point, he simply vanished. And that was the end of that.)

Roys Oatman had a decision to make: he could stay with Brewster at Socorro Peak, or he could forge ahead toward the bill of goods he'd been sold in California. In what was one more in a series of bad decisions (starting with the decision to align with Brewster at all), Oatman decided on California. He, his family, and twenty others continued the onward journey to their vision of the promised land.

It wasn't a pretty sight. As one historian wrote, "Their situation was desperate. Their horse had died, and their scant remaining cattle were so weak that some of the children, aged two to seventeen, had been forced to walk [for] long stretches. . . . They were on a barely blazed trail eroded by recent storms. The food they'd packed under the floor of their prairie schooners before starting west was nearly spent. . . . They had abandoned one of their wagons in New Mexico after their oxen had dwindled to the point where they had no way to pull it."[1]

By the time the handful of emigrants reached the Mexican settlements in Arizona, things had deteriorated even more, if you can believe it. (Never say things could never get worse, because you'll find out *exactly* how much worse they can get.) They were down to scant fodder for their animals; in their starving condition, the teams were barely able to stand in the scorching heat. The settlements the party came to either had little food to spare or had been deserted as a result of Indian raids—you know, those peaceful Indians who had no disposition for war.

Just when you'd think the only way was up, things got even worse. By then, as you can easily imagine, Roys Oatman had just about had it. He was responsible for a wife and seven children at a point where his animals were dying and the food was all but gone. He became difficult and quarrelsome—so much so that most of the other travelers split off and went their own way. Only two other families elected to keep traveling with Oatman, who assumed command of the small party.

The plucky pioneers finally reached Tucson in January 1851. From there, they forged ahead in the direction of the Gila River, at that point a hundred miles from the Colorado and the confluence that had been touted as Brewster's Land of Bashan.

Somewhere along the path, the three lonely wagons practically tripped over a Pima Indian village. A proud and industrious people, the Pima were known for being generous to white settlers who were passing by. (Maybe *these* were the peaceful folk Brewster had envisioned.) The Pimas warned the travelers that the trail ahead was treacherous and almost impassable. They also warned of hostile Indians who roamed the territory. According to the Pima, going on would be at the risk of their very lives. The other two families, figuring the Indians had a firm grip on reality, decided to stay among the Pima for a season. But not Oatman.

Oatman was not one to quit—especially so close to his goal. Despite the dire warnings of the Pima—who, by the way, decidedly did know what they were talking about—Oatman figured that within a few days, he would arrive at Fort Yuma on the California side of the Colorado River, where he could refresh his supplies and get a new start. He decided to push ahead. It would be the final bad decision of his life.

As close as he was to his goal, it remained a ghastly journey. The Oatmans had two yoke of cattle and one yoke of oxen, all of which were dying in their tracks. A newsman of the day later described Arizona as "a barren, deserted, dreary waste, useful only as a dwelling place for the coyote." Roys Oatman undoubtedly would have agreed with that dreary assessment. As he doggedly plowed onward, he was on the edge of a complete breakdown.

Oatman pushed his family to travel at night so they could avoid the worst of the desert sun. The oxen were so weary that each time they reached a hill, the Oatmans had to completely unload the wagon, push and prod the exhausted oxen to the top, then go back and fetch all the supplies and carry them back to the wagon. It was grueling. The only thing that kept him going was Mary Ann, who continually reassured him that they would make it.

Maybe Salt Lake City—even with Brigham Young in the bargain—wasn't looking so bad after all.

At last—on February 18, 1851—they arrived at the Gila River, approximately ninety miles from present-day Yuma, Arizona.[2] They pulled the wagon to an island in the middle of the shallow water, rejoicing at having safely arrived. All day long the children babbled happily as they played in and around the wagon and splashed in the shallow waters. At one point the children started animatedly discussing what they'd do if attacked by Indians. Fifteen-year-old Lorenzo, puffing his chest out, proclaimed that he would get a gun and fight the Indians off. At seven, little Mary Ann declared that she would run away. And Olive? Olive shuddered at the very thought, vowing she would kill herself before "falling into the hands of the savages."

Famous last words.

Late that afternoon, Roys Oatman climbed onto a large stone and sat gazing despondently into the distance. For as far as the eye could see in every direction was nothing but arid mesas, dust, alkali, and rocky canyons. The only sign of life was an occasional lizard skittering through the dust. It was nothing like what the pioneers arriving in Salt Lake saw laid out before them.

As the sun started dipping below the horizon, Oatman finally had the breakdown that had been threatening for days. He buried his face in his hands and sobbed until he was shaking from head to toe. His concerned wife and children ran to where he sat, moaning and howling with despair. Upon seeing Mary Ann, he cried, "Mother, Mother, in the name of God, I know something terrible is about to happen!"

He was right.

At sunset, the Oatmans unloaded the wagon once more before pushing it and their battered oxen to the other side of the river and up one last hill, preparing to move on to their final destination. Once the wagon and team were securely situated at the top of the hill, they retrieved their goods and started to reload the wagon.

In the gathering dark, fifteen-year-old Lorenzo was the first to see them—close to twenty shadowy figures creeping silently up the hill behind them. As he continued to watch, wide-eyed, he was gripped with horror to realize they were Apache warriors clad in wolf skins. (Some have theorized that they were actually Western Yavapai or Tolkepaya,[3] but for our purposes we'll go with Apache and leave the anthropological question to the experts.) The men appeared to be unarmed.

Lorenzo grabbed his father and pointed. After looking fairly uncertain for a minute or so, Roys quietly draped his arm over Lorenzo's shoulder and said, "Don't fear. The Indians will not hurt us."

Oatman stood his ground atop the hill and motioned for the Apaches to sit down and talk; they did, asking in Spanish for a pipe to smoke in friendship. Okay; so far, so good. A pipe was brought, lit up, and passed among the men. Everything seemed to be going well—and peacefully—until one of the Apache asked for food.

Nothing doing, Oatman replied. He simply couldn't spare any. After all, he didn't have enough to feed his family of nine— and even then, all he had left was beans and stale bread. The Apaches repeated their demands, growing increasingly furious and insistent.

Oatman may have made a series of blisteringly bad decisions, but he wasn't stupid. He knew he was out of options. Handing over hunks of the stale bread, he told the Apaches that their greed was effectively starving the Oatman family.

What Oatman couldn't have known is that the area had been suffering from a devastating drought and, of course, an associated famine. The Oatmans weren't alone in their fierce hunger—the Indians were starving too. And desperate times often call for desperate measures. Little could Oatman have realized exactly how desperate things were about to get.

The Indians shuffled off a slight distance before sitting down and gobbling up the bread. Relief washed over Oatman as he heard them talking among themselves in their native tongue; the immediate danger had passed. Or so it *seemed*. Oatman told his family to finish reloading the wagon as fast as they could so they could get on their way. Mary Ann climbed into the wagon and packed away the items her husband and children handed up to her.

Suddenly a blood-curdling cry split the still night air. The astonished family watched, frozen with fear, as the Apaches pulled short, thick clubs from beneath their wolf skins and charged. Lorenzo took the first blow to the head; falling to the ground and bleeding profusely, he was left for dead. Within seconds his father was surrounded and beaten to death. Two of the Indians grabbed Olive and Mary Ann, dragging them to one side while the rest of the family was slaughtered before their eyes. Mrs. Oatman died from a crushed skull, still clutching her baby boy in her arms.

Almost as quickly as it had begun, the attack was over. Olive later wrote that as she struggled against the Apache who strong-armed her, she could hear "the groans of my poor mother." She then watched the rest of the Indians ransack the wagon for what little was left, breaking open trunks, discarding what they didn't want, and tearing the canvas from the top of the wagon. She saw them loot the bodies scattered on the ground, tearing boots and hats off her dead family members. She watched them steal the oxen and cattle. These were clearly the guys who gave Indians a bad name.

The Indians then moved quickly away—dragging Olive and Mary Ann down the hill, back across the shallow waters of the Gila and toward the west, where their village lay about a hundred miles away. The harsh desert floor quickly tore the skin of the girls' bare feet; they left bloody footprints on the ground as they struggled to keep up with their captors. Each time they started to fall behind, one of the men would yell "*Yokoa!*" and wave a war club menacingly in their direction. They may not have understood the word that escaped his lips, but they clearly understood the language of the club.

At last, Mary Ann collapsed into a heap on the ground. Surrounded by enraged Apaches, the little girl who earlier that day vowed she would run away from the Indians was kicked, prodded, and threatened, to no avail. She couldn't move a muscle. Finally, one warrior grabbed her feet, swung her into the air, and flung her across his back like a sack of grain. The group moved on.

Meanwhile, back at the wagon, the rest of the Oatmans lay dead—all except one, that is. Lorenzo, the first one attacked, had been *left* for dead, but he wasn't. He had been temporarily paralyzed by the blow to his head, but he remained conscious through the entire attack. He could feel an Apache yank the boots off his feet and rifle through his pockets. He could hear his sisters screaming as they were dragged off by the Indians, so he knew he was not the only survivor.

Bleeding copiously and unable to move, he vowed then and there that if it was the last thing he did, he would find and reclaim Olive and Mary Ann.

Hours after the Indians dragged his sisters off into the distance, Lorenzo was at last able to struggle to his feet, but he immediately toppled head-first down a deep gorge. For the next day, he suffered alternating periods of deep confusion and sharp awareness. He later said he was convinced his brains had been permanently knocked loose and were rattling around in his skull like so many marbles.

He had to have known that the odds against him were tremendous, but he finally managed to cross the Gila and wander along the trail in the direction the Indians had traveled. In his gravely injured condition, barefoot, and with no food or water, it was rough going. At one point, he had to fight off a pack of wolves by throwing rocks. By the third day, he was seriously considering gnawing off his own arm to relieve his hunger.

Suddenly, he heard the hooves of horses pounding against the desert floor.

He dropped to his knees, overwhelmed with relief at being saved.

Not so fast, Lorenzo.

The horsemen weren't rescuers, but Indians in red shirts, arrows notched in their bows. As his life flashed before him, one of the Indians leapt off his horse and ran toward Lorenzo, leaving his bow and arrow in the dust.

Seems it really *was* Lorenzo's lucky day: the Indians were two of the friendly Pima from the village at Maricopa Wells. Lorenzo later recalled, "He embraced me with every expression of pity and condolence that would throb in an American heart." The pair hoisted Lorenzo onto one of the horses and carried him back to their village, where they nursed him back to health. Two weeks later, they carried him to Fort Yuma—the place his father had been trying to reach.

Three days into the journey to Fort Yuma, they came across the bodies of Lorenzo's slain family members. There was no way to dig a grave in the rocky, volcanic soil, so they simply gathered the bodies together into a single "grave"[4] and piled rocks over them to dissuade foraging animals. (According to the Oatman family genealogy, the remains were moved and reburied several times before finally being buried in the river by early Arizona colonizer Charles Poston.)

Lorenzo's wanderings may have been rough, but his sisters weren't doing any better. They were forced to walk across the desert for two days and two nights without rest. The only occasional stops were for rushed meals—and the fare they were given paled in comparison to the meager food they'd had earlier along the trail. The Indians gave them nothing more than burnt dough, beans, and a bit of stringy beef.

On the morning of the third day, they finally came to a village consisting of about three hundred Tonto Apaches who lived in half-buried, thatched huts. Upon seeing the girls, a crowd of Indians rushed toward them, shrieking, spitting in their faces, and dancing around them. With that, Olive and Mary Ann got a preview of what their lives would be like—and Olive expected to be killed.

They weren't killed, but that might have been easier compared to what *did* happen. Both girls were called *Onatas* and were given the status of slaves. Frequently beaten and mistreated, they were expected to lug water, fetch firewood, forage for food, and perform other menial tasks. As Olive described it, the Indians "took unwarranted delight in whipping us on beyond our strength."

Right away, Olive could see that women in general had little status in the tribe—and the women slaves fared worst of all. Standard fare for the Apache men was a mush or gruel of boiled meat, generally snake, ground squirrel, or venison. Not so for the women, especially Olive and Mary Ann. They spent almost every waking moment looking for any vegetation they could use to stave off hunger: cactus root, wild onion, prickly pear fruit, and yucca buds. It was a meager diet at best and did little to sustain the physical labor expected of the girls.

So it continued for more than a strenuous, backbreaking year—and it might have gone on forever had not a band of

Mohave Indians living two hundred miles to the north visited the Apache village in early March 1852. Spying the two girls, Mohave tribal chief Espaniola proposed a trade: two horses, three blankets, some beads, and a basket of vegetables for Olive and Mary Ann.

Just like that, the two girls were property of the Mohave. On that same day, they left with their new masters, a Mohave war party along with Espaniola's young daughter Topeka. As they started out on the rigorous journey, Olive and Mary Ann were each given a small piece of beef. For the next ten punishing days, all they had to eat were the roots they were allowed to dig along the way.

On the morning of the eleventh day, Olive delighted at the beauty of their destination: a lush, green valley with groves of cottonwood trees and small fields of wheat surrounding the flowing waters of the Colorado River. Ironically, the village was at the confluence of the Gila and Colorado, near present-day Needles, California—Brewster's (and therefore Roys Oatman's) coveted "Land of Bashan." Olive couldn't help but notice the area's stark contrast to the arid wasteland in which she'd been living for the previous year.

She may have loved the landscape, but Olive initially struggled with the Mohave, whom she at first described as "fierce" and "filthy-looking." Those feelings didn't last long. Where she and her sister were treated abominably by the Apaches, she actually developed a familial relationship with Chief Espaniola (his non-Mohave name); his wife, Aespaneo; and their daughter, Topeka—people for whom Olive expressed great affection during the years after her captivity. In fact, Olive and Mary Ann were "adopted" into the family, given the clan name *Oach*, and given a small plot of land to garden. Olive was given the nickname "Spantsa." The term the Mohaves used to describe them, *ahwe*, meant "stranger" or "enemy"—not "captive" or "slave."[5]

Names aside and despite finding true sympathy and affection from Topeka, the girls were still treated like slaves in many ways—not only by the adults, but by the children. Olive remembered her time as one of drudgery, saying she "soon learned that our condition was that of unmitigated slavery." Each morning both girls were roused early from their blankets and sent out in search of mesquite seed—ground up and boiled in water, it was a major food of the Mohave. Olive's disdain for it was clear. She called the sour mixture "mesquite mush," said it was tasteless, and complained that it churned in her stomach.

There *were* also some happy moments. The delighted Mohaves often asked the girls to sing for them, rewarding them afterward with gifts of beads and scraps of red flannel. Olive and Mary Ann dabbled with some Mother Goose songs but most often sang Sunday school hymns.

As had also happened among the Apaches, the Mohaves peppered the girls with constant questions about white customs, traditions, and beliefs. The Indians were especially ribald about the girls' explanations of their religious beliefs, which elicited shrieks of laughter from the Indians. "When you go up to your heaven," one squaw jeered, "you had better take a strong piece of bark and tie yourself up, or before long you will be falling down among us again."

Accounts of what happened over the next few months vary. Olive later said she was too terrified to try to escape. In other accounts, she said that she and her sister often whispered about the hope of escaping, even discussing some rudimentary plans. Some say that she likely had Stockholm Syndrome, a condition in which a captive develops a loyalty to and affection for her captors and thus never attempts escape.

Regardless of which was true, escape seemed pretty unlikely. After all, they no longer really knew where they were. The nearest white settlements may as well have been thousands of miles away, and the memory of their eleven-day trek across the unyielding desert was fresh in their minds, something they couldn't imagine repeating. In fact, when a large group of whites visited the Mohaves while she was there, Olive didn't even try to contact them—let alone leave with them.[6] You'll see why later.

And then came the famous tattoo.

Some say the tattoo was given to Olive to mark her as a slave and prevent any dash for freedom, but that seems unlikely, since historians say that most Mohave women at that time had tattoos on their chins.[7] In actuality, those historians say, Olive was tattooed as a mark of acceptance into the tribe—the tattoos were considered by the Mohave as a form of identification crucial in the afterlife, allowing them to enter the land of the dead and be recognized by their ancestors.[8]

Both Olive and Mary Ann were tattooed on their arms, and both received the blue cactus chin tattoo. Whatever the purpose for the tattoos, it doesn't sound like much fun. Olive described the process as one in which they "pricked the skin in small regular rows on our chins with a very sharp stick, until they bled freely." The sticks were then dipped in weed juice and powdered blue turquoise, which was then pressed into the pinpricks on the chin.

Olive accepted her tattoo, as she did most other aspects of the Mohave. Think about it: she believed the rest of her family was dead. Here, she had at least the semblance of a family. After entertaining some initial fantasies of escape, she eventually accepted the fact that she wouldn't be trekking across the desert again. Resigned, she and her sister decided to do their best to blend in. They learned the Mohave language, dressed according to Mohave tradition, and adopted Mohave habits.

They had become, for all intents and purposes, Mohave.

A year or so later, tragedy struck. There had been no rain for almost a year, and the meager crops of the Mohave failed. Even the mesquite seeds were rapidly vanishing. The tribe lapsed into starvation. Olive was able to maintain some strength, but Mary Ann had never recovered from her forced marches across the desert. She weakened at an alarming rate. Desperate to save her sister, Olive frantically searched for edible roots and blackbird eggs, but most of what she found was confiscated by the Mohave to feed their own dying children.

Mary Ann became unable to move and spent her days lying in the shade of a cottonwood tree, deliriously singing songs to herself. She was not alone; many in the village were weakened to the point of death. Late one evening, Mary Ann whispered, "Olive, I shall die soon. You will live and get away." All too soon she wasted completely away, Olive recalled, "as sinks the innocent infant to sleep in its mother's arms."9

Many members of the tribe died as a result of the famine. Traditionally, the Mohave burned their dead. Horrified by that thought, Olive appealed to her adopted mother, Aespaneo, who got permission from her husband for the ten-year-old child to be buried instead. Olive dug a shallow grave for her sister in the little garden they had tilled together. In her third year of captivity, Olive Oatman found herself alone among the Indians—"the only time," she later recalled, "in which, without any reserve, I really hoped to die."10

That may have happened, in fact, had it not been for the kindness of Aespaneo, who slipped Olive a handful of cornmeal—part of the tribe's last reserves. Along with a little mesquite soup, it kept Olive alive. By spring 1854, fish started appearing in a nearby lake, and refreshing rains overflowed the Colorado. The drought had ended.

But don't think Olive was in the clear. Far from it.

Within a few months, war broke out between the Mohave and the Cocopah, a large tribe headquartered seven hundred miles away. Olive was immediately informed of a horrifying Mohave custom: whenever one of their warriors died in battle, a prisoner was sacrificed to soothe the warrior's angry spirit. Olive knew she was the only captive in the village. For five long months, she was plagued by constant fear, certain she would be sacrificed any day. Then the miracle came: the war ended. The Mohave triumphed over their much more numerous enemies without losing a single warrior. Olive remembered, "I buried my face in my hands and silently thanked God."11

And that did it. At that point, Olive resigned herself to "conciliate the best wishes of all" and do nothing to aggravate anyone. Setting aside any hopes of rescue or escape, she settled into life with the Mohave, cheered by the continuing friendship of Aespaneo and Topeka.

Escape, in fact, became a somewhat hilarious notion. At this point, the Mohaves told her she was free to leave whenever she wanted to, but there was an important caveat: they would not escort her to the nearest white settlement. They feared retribution for having kept Olive for so long. So there was Olive, who didn't own a horse and didn't know the way, told she'd have to make a go of it on her own. Clearly, she wasn't leaving—or "escaping," as some would call it.

But neither did she grab the opportunity when a group of white men showed up in February 1854. Almost two hundred strong, they were members of the Whipple Expedition who were surveying for a railroad route, and they stayed among the Mohave for *a week*. During the week, Olive literally hid out. She didn't approach even one of the men to ask if they could help her back to white society.[12] It seems that by then, at least, Olive was satisfied with her station in life. It's almost certain she considered herself assimilated.

That might have been the end of it all, with Olive living out her days in quiet complacency among the Mohave, except for one thing.

Remember Lorenzo?

He hadn't given up on his quest to rescue his sisters.

In the ensuing years since being rescued by the Pima, he had been trying one desperate scheme after another to find Olive and Mary Ann. (We, of course, know it was too late for Mary Ann, but Lorenzo didn't have a clue.) He tried demanding justice from local officials in California. He joined up with various parties of miners who were exploring southern California, hoping to steer them toward Arizona. He tried pleading with strangers.

In 1854, hearing that a new garrison had arrived at Fort Yuma, Lorenzo sent a letter asking the army for help. The reply flabbergasted him: Yes, there were two white girls being held captive by the Mohave, he was told, but gosh—no one quite knew what to do about it.

What?

Lorenzo leaped into action, involving the media. He wrote the editor of the *Los Angeles Star* about the whole thing; the *Star* responded with an editorial lambasting the army as a pack of cowards and incompetents. Simultaneously, Lorenzo petitioned California's governor to intervene. The governor was more than willing to help, he responded, but he had no authority. He suggested that Lorenzo contact the Indian Department in Washington. Weary of all the runaround, Lorenzo was in the process of drawing up a petition to send to the feds when he learned that the *Star* editorial had been more effective than anyone could have anticipated, thanks to some fancy fictionalizing.

Long story short, late in January 1856, Henry Grinnell—a carpenter at Fort Yuma—read the article about two captive white girls to a Yuma Indian named Francisco. But Henry didn't stop when the article did. Knowing Francisco couldn't read English, he continued on, weaving a fantastic ending claiming that the president of the United States had ordered five million soldiers to surround the Mohave Valley. The US soldiers were going to slaughter every Indian living there unless the Oatman girls were released unharmed, Grinnell "read."[13]

Wide-eyed, Francisco proceeded to cough up the information. He knew where two white girls *had* been among the Mohave, he said, but one was dead. In exchange for four blankets and some beads, he offered to return in twenty days with the remaining white girl. (Looks like those Indian blankets held a *lot* of sway in the day.)

Grinnell took Francisco to the fort's commander, and the deal was struck. Grinnell himself offered to make sure the beads and four blankets would be on hand. On February 8, Francisco and three companions set out for the Mohave village.

Scarcely able to anticipate what was about to happen, Olive Oatman, now nineteen years old, was innocently digging groundnuts one morning when she heard a man named Francisco had come to rescue her. The next thing she knew, she was seized and confined to the chief's *ki* (dwelling) so the tribal council could debate the terms of her release.

And there she stayed confined for three long days. She later said she had little faith in the council—she viewed them as a bunch of aimless, wild maniacs.[14] After three days of wondering whether the Mohave would simply kill her and be done with the whole thing, she was led outside and plastered with mud, giving her a "dun, dingy color, unlike that of any race I ever saw."[15] Next she was ordered to speak nothing but gibberish—and threatened with immediate death if she did anything to give Francisco the notion that she was an American. Because, of course, the Mohave had told Francisco she was *not* an American, but from a race of people similar to the Indians who had come from a distant land.

The charade went on for several more days. Finally, Francisco upped the ante: he offered blankets in exchange for Olive. He then presented Olive with a note, the first written communication she had seen in five years. It was proof that Francisco had come from the commanding lieutenant colonel to obtain Olive.

At that point, the floodgates opened. Olive spoke in clear and flawless English, telling Francisco about being smeared with mud and forced to speak gibberish, all in an attempt to trick him. Furious, the Yuma said that if the Mohave refused to release Olive, they could take up the issue with a band of white soldiers who would arrive in his stead.

Reaction among the Mohave was mixed. Some wanted to kill Olive and end the dispute then and there. Some were eager to fight the soldiers. Most just wanted to take what they could get in exchange for Olive, send her back to the fort, and wash their hands of the whole ordeal. In the end, Espaniola demanded that a white horse be thrown into the deal and that Topeka be able to accompany Olive to Fort Yuma. He wanted to make sure the Yuma didn't steal Olive for themselves. And so it was settled.

The next morning, Olive ate her last breakfast of mesquite mush. Before leaving with her traveling companions, she hung back at the grave of her sister. As Olive pined, Mary Ann "had come with me to that lonely exile; and now I felt what it was to know she could not go with me from it."[16] Olive wanted to take her scraps of cloth and beads, especially those that had been worn by Mary Ann, but the Mohave adamantly refused. They said she could take with her only the garment she wore—a skirt fashioned of bark. She managed to smuggle out as a souvenir a small jar of the groundnuts she had been gathering for the previous five years.

After the extremities of a twenty-day journey, Olive found herself on the edge of civilization. Ready to board the ferry that would take her to the fort, she hesitated: she was wearing nothing above the waist, which was Mohave traditional dress, and she didn't want to arrive half-naked in nothing but her bark skirt. After some swift negotiation, an officer's wife sent a brightly colored party dress for the young woman to wear.

On the morning of February 28, 1856, the entire garrison at Fort Yuma turned out to give the brightly clad girl a resounding welcome, cannons and guns firing a salute as she was returned to "her people." But far from being elated at her release, Olive was for several days incoherent. What didn't seem to cross anyone's mind, including hers, was the fact that recovered captives are often forced to live in two worlds, rejected by both. There was nothing easy about the road ahead. It had been five years and ten days since Olive had been abducted by the Apache.

Then came the most jaw-dropping, unbelievable news of all: Olive learned that the brother she assumed dead was actually the one who had engineered her release. Within a few days, Lorenzo arrived at Fort Yuma for his long-awaited reunion with his sister; their meeting made newspaper headlines across the country. At first, Lorenzo barely recognized Olive. At that point she mostly refused to speak, and when she did, she seemed to have trouble remembering the English language, even though she had spoken clearly to Francisco just days earlier. But that's not all—following years of unrelenting exposure to the sun, her skin was brown and burnt.[17] She no longer resembled the sister who had been dragged away the night of the massacre.

As for Olive, she became an instant celebrity, described by the *Los Angeles Star* as "a pretty girl" who had been "disfigured by tattooed lines on her chin." The story in the *Star*—sensational to the detail—played on the emotions of readers who were both horrified and fascinated with Olive's captivity. One *Star* article mused, "What were her sensations, during all this time, must be imagined; for she is not, as yet, able to express her thoughts in language."[18]

It didn't take Olive and Lorenzo long to renew their affection as siblings. Together they went first to California, then to Jackson County in southern Oregon, where they moved in with some Oatman cousins.

As you can imagine, Olive attracted constant attention because of the striking tattoo on her chin—including the attention of Methodist minister Royal Byron Stratton, who exploited Olive by penning a sensationalized book about the massacre of her family and her subsequent life with the Indians. You have to remember that Americans of that day relished the image of Indians—*all* Indians—as bloodthirsty, reckless savages, and Stratton played skillfully to his audience. As one historian pointed out, however, "As hard as Stratton tried to twist her story into an indictment of the 'degraded bipeds' who raised her, Olive's love for the Mohave bleeds through the pages of Stratton's book, and it is also clear in the interview she gave soon after her ransom."[19]

Titled *Life among the Indians* when it was first published in San Francisco in 1857—and later retitled *Captivity of the Oatman Girls*—the book was rife with misinformation and filled with long passages of anti-Indian material. Eager readers gobbled it up, of course, and it became a runaway bestseller, selling more than thirty thousand copies. It was subsequently reprinted in both San Francisco and New York and sold out of three separate editions.

Spurred on by the book's success, Olive went to the eastern United States on a multiyear lecture tour in 1858, during which she spoke to packed houses. While the long sleeves of her dresses covered the tattoos on her arms, the blue tattoo on her chin was readily obvious and caused universal excitement and curiosity among her audiences.

As her lecture tour began, Olive was relatively gentle when referring to the Mohaves who had held her captive. As time went on, however, she grew increasingly negative toward them— strengthening the belief of many that she had suffered from Stockholm Syndrome during the time she was with the Mohave.

The more time elapsed since her rescue, the harsher her feelings became and the less empathy or positive feelings she expressed for the Indians.

As rigorous as the lecture tour was, one good thing came out of it: Between the proceeds from the book and her lecture tour, she and Lorenzo were able to pay for their advanced education at the prestigious University of the Pacific.

Oh, make that two good things: While she was on the lecture circuit in Farmington, Michigan, in 1864, she met John Brant Fairchild, a New York-born cattleman and farmer. The two married in Rochester, New York, in November 1865.

By all accounts, the two seemed to be happy, moving into a stately two-story house in Sherman, Texas. They adopted a baby girl, Mary Elizabeth, and called her Mamie. In an effort to distance Olive from her troubled past, Fairchild burned all the copies of Stratton's book that he could get his hands on and put a halt to Olive's lecture tours.

Despite those efforts, Olive apparently did continue to be haunted by her past. Though her husband was one of the most prominent businessmen in Sherman, Olive rarely left the house. When she did, she was extremely shy and attempted to cover her chin tattoo with heavy makeup, tinted face powders, and dark veils. She periodically left Fairchild and their home in Sherman to seek treatment for "nervous ailments," once going as far away as Canada to admit herself to a medical spa for three months. In her forties, she battled debilitating headaches and depression. Letters found after her death bear stark evidence to the psychological scars that remained throughout her life. Today, we would call her condition post-traumatic stress disorder (PTSD), a condition she never overcame.[20]

The PTSD wasn't the only thing that plagued Olive. There were rumors—amazingly, started by her childhood friend Susan Thompson—that Olive's sadness and grief upon returning to white civilization had a specific source. Thompson claimed that Olive had been married to a Mohave and had borne him two sons. That speculation is a matter of considerable scholarly debate.[21] Most scholars and historians reject that notion. For one thing, once Olive married Fairchild, the couple resorted to adoption because she was unable to bear children. For another, a Mohave historian said if such a thing had happened, "we would all know"—her sons would have been mixed-race Mohave who would have stood out and been easily traced to her. And for still another, half a century after her release, anthropologist A. L. Kroeber interviewed a Mohave named Musk Melon who had known Olive well. He said nothing about her having been married or having borne children.[22] Those who believe that Olive may have been married or had children point to her Mohave nickname as evidence. Apparently the nickname "Spantsa" implied sexual promiscuity.

But perhaps we should most seriously consider the evidence that comes straight from the horse's mouth, as it was. Throughout her life, Olive herself steadfastly denied ever having been married to a Mohave or ever having been raped or sexually mistreated—by either the Apache *or* the Mohave. In fact, she pledged, "to the honor of these savages let it be said, they never offered the least unchaste abuse to me."[23]

Let's face it: we may never know the whole story of what happened to Olive during her time with the Indians. We *do* know that she never quite rid herself of the memories—or the affections, for that matter. Late in her life she traveled to New York City to meet the Mohave leader Irataba; there she affectionately spoke with him about old times.[24] And throughout her life she kept her jar of groundnuts, which we would recognize as hazelnuts.

As the years passed, rumors circulated that Olive, unable to assimilate back into white life, went mad and died in an insane asylum. Not true. Despite her probable PTSD, she lived a full, long (at least for those days) life, dying of a heart attack on March 20, 1903, at the age of sixty-five. Her husband died four years later on April 25, 1907. They are both buried in an elaborate grave at West Hill Cemetery in Sherman, Texas. A Texas historical marker was placed on the grave in 1969.

But guess who *did* end up in an insane asylum in Hartford, Connecticut? Royal B. Stratton, Olive's imaginative biographer, who died there in 1875.

Now that you know the story, you might notice Olive's name cropping up here and there. The tragic girl with the blue tattoo apparently lives on in a plethora of formats. For example, the area where the family met their demise on the south bank of the Gila River is now known as Oatman Flat. The town of Oatman, Arizona—a ghost town recently revived by tourists from a nearby gambling town—is named in her honor and is located twenty-five miles southwest of Kingman. Its chief claim to fame—besides its connection to Olive herself—is that Hollywood greats Clark Gable and Carole Lombard spent their honeymoon there at the Oatman Hotel. (And let's face it: lots more people have heard of Gable and Lombard than of Olive.)

Speaking of Hollywood, Olive's story was the subject of "The Lawless Have Laws," a 1965 episode of *Death Valley Days* in which future president Ronald Reagan starred as Lieutenant Colonel Burke. In the episode, Burke led Lorenzo, played by Tim McIntire, on the search for his sister.

Olive is also the subject of an Elmore Leonard story, two novels, and four children's books—including a Christian title that is sold with a collectible Olive Oatman figurine. Not that we think her story—replete with massacre, abduction, and forced captivity—seems necessarily appropriate for children . . .

unanimously adopted with a
er and the delegation adjourned.
he state committee had a brief
ion. There were only a few ab-
ees. W. P. Phillips was in Ros-
leton's place and R. I. Sharkey in
n D. Post's. M. J. Dady did not
an alternate.

here were two vacancies caused by
death of Hugh McRoberts and W.
lenn, and G. J. Smith served in
ert Hasbrouck's absence. The
mittee heard no contests and eu-
ed the temporary roll of the con-
ion for the permanent organiza-

muel Ely Quigg of New York was
ted for temporary chairman of the
ention and the hour of the first
on was set for 12 o'clock on Tues-
The committee then adjourned.

far as could be learned nothing
een settled in the way of a can-
e for secretary of state. James
cEwen, Anson G. McCook and
McDonough are mentioned, while
date Mongin still is in the race.
s said that the position would be
d to Kings county today.

advocates of canal improvement
nd discussed plans for the canal
in the platform. They could not
on what form the resolution
be put in, but it was the con-
of opinion that a 1,000-ton barge

he was William Hooper Young after
he had been positively identified by
Mac Levy, an instructor of physical
culture, in whose establishment in

WILLIAM HOOPER YOUNG.

Brooklyn, Young was at one time em-
ployed.

Detectives sent to Derby reported

was talking with You
ance of the latter, Dix
boken, passed by the
in. Mr. Anzer, who
business partner of Yo
what in doubt about t
of Young, but as he w
oner raised his head
"Hello, there's Anzy."

While Mr. Levy's i
Young and the latter's
cleared up all uncerta
the case the police ha
for several hours tha
man they wanted.

Young was shown a
blegram sent by his
Young, from Paris, a
surrender and declarin
would stand by him.

Young read the m
rolled down his cheek
to the wall of his cell
a strong effort to repr
refused to speak of th

PRESIDENT IN

Reviewed an Immense
to Spanish War

Detroit, Sept. 23.—
dent Roosevelt partici
viewed the military p
the greatest demonstr
ever seen in the city

Newspaper with image of William Hooper Young—who did, after all, make
the news.

WILLIAM HOOPER YOUNG
AN APPLE THAT FELL FAR FROM THE TREE

ON SEPTEMBER 18, 1902, THE body of a woman named Anna Nilsen Pulitzer was found in the Morris Canal just outside Jersey City, New Jersey. Anna had obviously fallen on bad times. Her skull was fractured in two places, and she had been stabbed in the abdomen. That's not all: a twenty-pound weight was attached to a leather strap around her waist.

And if you're wondering why Anna is featured in this book, listen to this—it was a *Mormon* who did it to her.

The story actually starts with Brigham Young (no, it wasn't *him*, heaven forbid). After Brigham's first wife died in 1832, he married Mary Ann Angell. Their sixth child and third son was a strapping baby boy named John Willard Young, who was born on October 1, 1844, in Nauvoo, Illinois. (It wasn't John Willard, either, but this is an important part of the back story, so stick with us.)

Like lots of babies born about that time in Nauvoo, John Willard became a pioneer early in his life, crossing the vast prairie (likely in his mother's arms or in the bed of a wagon) to the Salt Lake Valley. There his father put down roots and started the work to establish Zion.

Legend has it (from a number of very reliable sources) that John Willard was Brigham Young's favorite son. There could have been a number of reasons for his favored status. One reason is that John Willard was Brigham's first son to be born under the covenant, as the endowment that led to the sealing had been revealed in Nauvoo.[1]

He may also have been Brigham's favorite because as he grew, he shared lots of the same qualities that made his famous father a legend. He was intelligent, cultured, witty, charismatic, and charming— the kind of boy *any* father would favor. He was clearly the most articulate and charismatic of Brigham Young's fifty-nine children, a considerable feat in itself. Unfortunately, however, John Willard also had some qualities all his own: John Willard was dependent, entitled, lazy, careless, and impulsive.[2] Well, boys will be boys.

Focused on John Willard's positive traits, Brigham Young made sure that his son had the best of everything, including the best formal education available and multiple opportunities to travel and experience life outside Zion. As a result, John Willard had an astute understanding of business, American politics, and other important issues of his day.[3]

John Willard was also ordained an Apostle, which in itself wasn't that unusual, considering his heritage. What *was* unusual was that he was both an Apostle and a member of the First Presidency without ever having been a member of the Quorum of the Twelve. What's also unusual is that he spent most of his adult life in New York City, away from the center of Zion.

On with the story—and the link to Mrs. Pulitzer, whose body was found in the Morris Canal . . . and that takes us to John Willard's son, William Hooper Young. He may have been Brigham Young's grandson, but *this* was an apple that fell far from the tree, so to say.

William Hooper Young was born in Philadelphia, Pennsylvania, on March 13, 1871. His mother, Elizabeth Canfield Young (Libbie), was visiting there when Hooper, as he was called, elected to make his appearance; his father, John Willard Young, was in Utah.[4] If you think it a bit strange that a woman about to give birth had traveled so far from her home and husband, you may be right—by the time Hooper was ten, his parents had divorced.

John Willard stayed in Salt Lake City, at least initially, where he fulfilled the duties of an Apostle in the Church. On the other hand, Libbie married a non-Mormon, moved to Seattle, and there raised a nice non-Mormon family. Hooper stayed in Utah, though it's not quite known with whom he lived. There is some evidence that he may have briefly studied chemistry at Provo's Brigham Young Academy. An old friend recalled that "even in those bygone days Hooper had funny streaks, and would often surprise the boys with his statements or actions."

According to his stepfather, he was sent to military school but ran away. The stepfather also hinted that Hooper's "difficult" ways had caused more than a little bitterness between him and Hooper's mother. But he felt compelled to publicly defend his wife, saying, "She was always a good mother, and any statement made by . . . her former husband [John Willard Young] to the effect that she exercised a bad influence upon young [Hooper] is absolutely and unequivocally false."[5]

As for Libbie, she defended herself by saying that John Willard had himself "damaged" Hooper. First of all, she alleged, he sent Hooper off to work on a cattle ranch all by himself when he was only a child. He followed that up, she claimed, by forcing Hooper to work on the railroad at the tender age of eighteen, in effect rendering him homeless. She also told anyone who wanted to listen that Hooper's brother was in jail for robbery. But that's a story for another day.

Sounds like the typical divorce: accusations flying in every direction.

Regardless of what really happened in those years following the divorce, let's just say that Hooper wasn't very popular with his extended family. Some relatives said he was weak-minded and deranged. Others described him as a drifter and a bum. One cousin said that Hooper was "a bright young man, but very erratic"; still others said he was a morphine addict.

Despite his obvious problems, Hooper was ordained an elder. He was called to England as a missionary in 1890; while there is no record of specific problems, his name ceased to appear in any mission records less than a year after he arrived in England. It seems he left the mission holding the bag and joined his father's family in London; together, they traveled on an extended trip to Paris. They finally returned to London, but Hooper never finished his mission or even resumed any of his missionary activities. Instead, he returned to the United States.

His cousins, who had nurtured such a dislike for him before, were none too happy to see him back home in 1893. For one thing, he had become rabidly anti-Mormon despite his heritage and his own missionary service. Looking back on his behavior during that period, one of his cousins described Hooper as "a strange fellow, having left home frequently to wander about the country like a tramp. He had an idea that he could become immensely wealthy by chance, and took numerous trips in the hope of a strike of fortune." There was even hushed talk that he had murdered someone in Salt Lake City soon after he arrived home.

He was hired as a reporter for the *Salt Lake Herald*, but that didn't last long. He became a chain smoker and a heavy drinker and became increasingly estranged from his family and the Church. Within a few months, Hooper pulled up stakes and left Utah; from then on, he became a wanderer.

His travels and his attempts at making a living were both varied and broad. He seemed to draw on his Salt Lake City newspaper experience for a time, briefly reporting for a paper in Washington, D.C., and working for a newspaper in San Francisco before publishing his own newspaper in Seattle. The Seattle paper was suppressed under anti-obscenity laws, and that's all we'll say about that; you can imagine the rest.

But there's no keeping a good man down. Hooper subsequently went on the road as a salesman for a drug company; peddled insurance; labored as a miner in Butte, Montana; and even became a cowboy in Arizona. During his travels, he lived in, among other places, San Francisco; Seattle; Portland; Chicago; New York City; Washington, D.C.; and Hoboken, New Jersey. It must have made for a staggering resume.

In addition to having a bevy of employers and trying out a broad variety of occupations, Hooper was a busy young man in a number of other ways. He became wanted for forgery. He fathered a daughter out of wedlock. And by 1900, he had become addicted to cocaine.

Hooper drifted to New York City in 1901, looked up two half-brothers, and borrowed money from them to support him in his travels (and to finance other things, it would be safe to suppose). He continued to contact other relatives, attempting to exploit them for whatever money he could get. Finally, the whole bunch of them threw their hands in the air, ceased all financial support, and completely cut off contact with Hooper. After all, he was interested only in their money—and when that stopped coming, so did he.

During much of the time Hooper crisscrossed the country, John Willard Young kept in touch with his errant son, making numerous attempts to help him. Finally, wearied and sickened by Hooper's debauched ways, John Willard also cut off all contact with his son. By then John Willard had leased a large apartment in New York City, where he was living; he refused to even allow Hooper to visit the apartment.

Speaking of John Willard, *that* was an interesting story all on its own. When he decided to lease the apartment in New York City, he "did not like close neighbors." So he actually leased three adjacent apartments overlooking Central Park and had them opened into one colossal apartment containing three "suites." It was far more space than he needed; he lived there alone with his daughter Mary and occasionally had one or two sons temporarily stay.

And his relationship with the Church in Manhattan has been described by one historian as a "peculiar" one.[6] When he was doing well financially, he regularly attended meetings and was generous with his tithes and offerings. When his wildly fluctuating finances were low, he shunned services but occasionally sent one of his sons to borrow $50 or $100 from the mission president, John G. McQuarrie. Nothing like using the local branch as your own personal thrift and loan.

In the spring of 1902, John Willard's business relocated him to Europe, an assignment that would last at least a year. Not wanting to give up his spacious apartment, he put mission president McQuarrie in charge of the real estate and invited four full-time missionaries working in Manhattan to occupy one of the three suites. President McQuarrie was to supervise the elders and keep an eye on the other two suites. It seemed like the ideal win-win situation. The four elders were happily settled in their suite before John Willard left for Europe.

No sooner had John Willard's ship drifted out of the harbor when an "obvious derelict" burst into President McQuarrie's office, begging for money from the mission.

"He introduced himself as Hooper Young," the surprised mission president later noted. "He claimed he was ill and too weak to work and needed to go to a sanitarium. He said he had no friends, and not even enough money to eat on. . . . It was not too difficult to diagnose his condition . . . [:] dissipation—including promiscuous association with women. . . ."[7]

President McQuarrie drew a line in the sand, but it wasn't as harsh as it could have been. He told Hooper that the Church could not use funds to assist "a derelict who chooses to follow an illicit, illegal, and indulgent life such as you are leading." With that, he could have—and, some might argue, *should* have—turned Hooper out onto the streets. After all, by that time Hooper had spent close to a decade bad-mouthing the Church.

Instead, President McQuarrie, without any input from the Europe-bound John Willard, told Hooper that his father had "left me in charge of three apartments. The four Elders working in this conference occupy one. You may have [a room] in either of the others." The arrangement was simple, straightforward, and fair: "The boys cook for themselves," President McQuarrie told Hooper. "You may share their meals. . . . I will pay your share. After a few days' rest you will . . . look for a job. I will give you enough to pay carfare—but nothing for dope or beer." McQuarrie was no dummy; he had Hooper all figured out within the first few minutes.

And so Hooper moved in sometime in June 1902. And things went pretty well . . . for a few weeks.

As President McQuarrie recalled, "I think at the time he was sincere in . . . his promises. He ate well and slept well, and after a week he went out each day looking for work." You'd think that with his amazing variety of job experience, Hooper could have found *something* for which he was qualified.

But that didn't happen. In fact, things started sliding down a slippery slope pretty rapidly. As President McQuarrie described it, "With the surge of increasing physical strength came also the lure of fixed habits, the carnal appetites. . . . His willpower was weak, his desires were strong."

And then things got worse than anyone could have anticipated. *So* much worse.

You see, very near John Willard's apartment—now being occupied by Mormon missionaries and Hooper Young—lived a couple named Joseph and Anna Pulitzer; they had married in Manhattan in November 1898. These two were a real piece of work. Joseph was a flashy dresser who was so flirtatious that most people were shocked when they found out he was married. But that didn't hold a candle to Anna, who was "well known in the Tenderloin district" and was described as "a very bad woman." She had already been arrested several times for solicitation—in other words, prostitution. Some are convinced that her husband, Joseph, was her pimp.

Remember the battered body of Anna Nilsen Pulitzer that was found in a New Jersey barge canal? One and the same—no less than our friendly neighborhood prostitute.

On the night of September 16, Hooper—with his "carnal appetites," as President McQuarrie described them—convinced Anna Pulitzer to come to his room, where he hired her. Just the follies one would want in an apartment where missionaries were living. After she performed the agreed-on deed, Hooper was in a pinch: he had no money to pay her for her services.

As he stalled, trying to figure out what to do, he gave her beer spiked with chloral hydrate—also called "knockout drops." Well, it knocked her out, all right. In fact, it knocked her out so thoroughly she seemed to stop breathing. She appeared to be dead.

As you can well imagine, Hooper panicked. Who wouldn't? After all, he was just trying to stall for time while he figured out what to do about his debt; he never *intended* to kill anyone. But now here she was, apparently dead. *Great.*

Hooper decided he would dismember the body and stash it in a trunk. That would at least buy him some more time; he could decide what to do with the trunk later. He dashed into his father's parlor and plucked a decorative Oriental scimitar off the wall. He boldly made the first cut—a six-inch gash across Anna's abdomen—but then lost courage.

But, wait—the knockout drugs *didn't* kill Anna. She was still alive, though very unconscious, when Hooper cut into her. As a result, she bled profusely while Hooper dragged her to the closet and stuffed her inside. There she bled to death.

Hooper made no attempt to clean up the apartment, but he did take a bath; there he sorted out his options and formulated a plan. He also splashed a lot of bloody water onto the walls and floor—including all over a shirt one of the missionaries had carelessly left on the floor. (Initially, that missionary was accused of the murder because of that shirt, but luckily things were quickly resolved. More about that later.)

Once he had cleaned himself up, Hooper decided to throw Anna's body in the New Jersey canal. The next twenty-four hours consisted of a flurry of activity for Hooper.

First, he pawned Anna's diamond earrings so he'd have cash to carry out the rest of his plan. Next, he bought a secondhand trunk. Finally, he rented a horse and buggy from a stable in Hoboken, New Jersey. Little did he realize he was leaving behind a trail of witnesses, but panic tends to overcome rational thought.

He steered the horse and buggy back to the apartment near Central Park and carried the trunk into his room. There, he folded Anna's body into the trunk and latched the trunk closed. Then he enlisted the help of the apartment building bellboy to strap the heavy trunk onto the buggy. Yet another witness.

Drawing the curtains of the buggy tightly closed, Hooper drove back to New Jersey and prepared to dump Anna's body into the barge canal. First, he had to figure out a way to keep her submerged. He came up with what *seemed* like a brilliant solution. Wrapping a leather strap around her waist, he removed a twenty-pound lead weight from the buggy and tied it to the strap (such weights were used to tether horses when the driver parked the buggy). When Hooper chucked the body into the canal, it sunk like a lead weight. Um, because it was tied to one.

Back at the apartment, Hooper realized he had to get rid of the evidence. He packed the trunk with all of the soiled clothing (hers and his), her false teeth (yum), her wig, and the pawn ticket that linked him to Anna's diamond earrings. Topping it all off with most of the soiled bedding, he drove the trunk to the train station. There he shipped the evidence to a fictitious person at a nonexistent address in Chicago.

That task completed, he returned the horse and buggy to the proprietor in Hoboken, got dressed up like a tramp, and disappeared.

The perfect crime?

Hardly. To begin with, Hooper didn't know anything about the ebbs and tides of the river, a detail that would prove disastrous to his plan.

Sure enough, two days later—on September 18—the tide ebbed, leaving the water only about six inches deep. It was hardly the ideal spot to hide a body. And there, mired face-down in the mud, was the nude, battered, and mutilated body of a blonde woman. The person who discovered her was the engineer of a trolley that ran between Newark and Jersey City; as soon as he saw the body, he immediately summoned the police.

Identification of the body was a lot faster than anyone could have hoped. You see, Joseph Pulitzer had reported his wife missing the morning after she disappeared. She had left their apartment after 11 p.m. to shop for a late supper, her husband said, but had never returned. Police in New York City who took the missing person report traced her to a fruit stand and a bakery but were unable to figure out where she went after that. Hearing about the body in New Jersey, Joseph rushed to the police station there. He identified the body immediately as that of his wife.

Now the police knew who the victim was, and they started working backward to gather witnesses and evidence. Both were readily and easily forthcoming. Seems Hooper hadn't thought out his plan well at all. The first clue was the lead weight; police effortlessly traced it to the livery in Hoboken where Hooper had rented the buggy. Sure enough, the livery owner identified it as one missing from a buggy he had rented out. The livery owner hadn't written down Hooper's name, but amazingly remembered him saying he had recently worked for a political newspaper in New Jersey. A visit to the paper's editor resulted in a staff photo; the livery owner readily pointed to Hooper as the man who had rented the buggy.

Busted.

It was all the evidence the police needed, but they nevertheless picked up more along the way to Hooper's apartment. The men who tended the bridge over the river had seen the buggy go by on the night in question, its curtains drawn tightly shut. And a New York City cab driver went to the police and told them he had driven Anna Pulitzer—like we said, she was "well-known"—and a mystery man to 103 West 58th Street, the address of John Willard's apartment.

Within twenty-four hours of finding the body, police had identified Hooper as the probable murderer, and they were chopping their way into John Willard Young's apartment.[8] Hooper wasn't there. But plenty of evidence of murder *was* there. There was blood *everywhere*, even under the kitchen sink and on the mattress. The police found empty beer bottles, one containing crystals of chloral hydrate. They also found the bloody scimitar. And that's not all. They found something particularly odd: a notebook with the words *blood atonement* scrawled at the top of the page; underneath were written a list of scriptures from the Bible.

And what of the four missionaries living in the apartment?

Picture this: They were singing a hymn before their evening prayers when they heard all the police commotion down the hall.[9] It can't have been what they were expecting. One of the elders looked into the hall and asked what was going on. In response, a gruff policeman ordered them to stay in their own suite.

Three of them did. But sensing trouble and knowing their proper chain of authority, they sent one elder diving out the window and scrambling down the fire escape. He ran the few blocks to the mission home and fetched President McQuarrie. The two of them ran back to the building, where an anxious and animated crowd gathered at the front entrance. President McQuarrie then realized the obvious: Hooper Young was involved in the murder that was already making headlines.

Drawing on their ingenuity, the two went to the rear of the building, clambered back up the fire escape, and went through the window into the suite where the three nervous missionaries were huddled. There the five held an impromptu and hasty mission conference. It was decided that the missionaries would answer every question completely and truthfully, no matter how repugnant, and that no one would provide any excuses for Hooper. Then they sat quietly and waited for the police to come knocking.

And come knocking they did. Before it was all over, the missionaries participated in multiple interviews with the police. They told police everything they knew about Hooper, his background, his behavior, and his movements. They insisted that no Mormon would hide or shelter him, even out of respect for his family. They made clear that the Church had told them to cooperate fully. Thanks to the *blood atonement* scribble, they were also pressed into explaining Mormon doctrine, which they did patiently and consistently. (A few weeks after the murder, a General Authority addressed the topic of blood atonement in general conference, further clarifying the Church's position.)

The missionary whose bloody shirt was found in the bathroom underwent insistent questioning as a possible accomplice to the murder. But he and the other three elders were soon officially cleared of any involvement.

The sensational headlines exploded nationwide: "Mormon Boy Murdered Mrs. Pulitzer in Obedience to Mormon Doctrine." Because of the Mormon connection, it was a headline and story that attracted immediate attention of Utah newspapers. People in Utah were also gripped by the fact that the murder took place in the apartment of an Apostle, the suspect was Brigham Young's grandson, and four missionaries shared the living space. You can just imagine the melee.

Police finally tracked down Hooper in Derby, Connecticut. He was agitated, nervous, inebriated on whiskey, and dressed like a hobo. At first he denied his identity, saying his name was Bert Edwards. Eventually he admitted who he was—partly because an old employer showed up at the jailhouse and identified him.

He may have admitted his identity, but that's where the truth ended. When questioned, he gave police a fantastic story about what had happened: there were actually *three* people in the apartment that night, he claimed—him, the unfortunate Anna Pulitzer, and a man named Charles Simpson Eiling. Everything was going along smoothly, Hooper said, until he left the apartment to go buy some whiskey.

When he got back, he said, Anna was dead. Eiling had murdered her.

Hooper said he decided to help Eiling hide the body and cover up the murder for a truly magnanimous purpose: he was afraid of embarrassing and disgracing his father, a Mormon Church Apostle, if the matter became public.

He admitted trying to cut up the body so he could fit it into a trunk, and also admitted that he lost bravado.[10] He did *not* admit to dumping the body in the canal but did say he knew that's what Eiling had done with the body.

And what of Eiling? Police did an extensive search for him. From what they could determine, he didn't exist. Oh, but grab this: the neighbors in the apartment building where Hooper lived—a curious and nosy bunch to be sure—told police they had seen Hooper shipping a trunk on the day after the murder. Police contacted the shipping company; records were checked. Hooper had shipped the trunk, all right, to a C. S. Eiling in Chicago. Lo and behold, there was no such person in Chicago, either.

Police in Chicago were on standby waiting for the arrival of the mysterious trunk. When it reached the city, they opened it. Inside, they found everything they needed to make the case against Hooper Young airtight.

Anna Pulitzer's body was taken to and buried in her old hometown—Perth Amboy, New Jersey—where her family still lived and remembered her as "a belle of Perth Amboy." And listen to this colorful detail: some people in Perth Amboy said that Anna had actually met Hooper Young when he blew through town nine years earlier as part of a band of Mormon missionaries. The residents had run the missionaries out of town, of course, but not before Anna and Hooper had "connected." At least, that's what the villagers claimed. And so when Anna decided to move to New York City a few weeks later, some thought she went in search of Hooper Young. No one knows for sure.

And what about Hooper? He pleaded not guilty by reason of insanity.

Hooper's murder trial began in New York City on February 4, 1903. His mother came from Seattle and stayed with former in-laws during the trial, appearing in court every day to support her son. His father did not attend the trial but wired money from Europe to pay for Hooper's defense attorney.

Determined to prove his insanity defense, Hooper put on quite a show for the reporters and jurors.[11] He stopped shaving, interrupted court proceedings to ask for a rabbit's foot, and often pretended to sleep through the trial. Six days into the trial the psychiatric experts who had been hired to determine his sanity proclaimed their opinion that he was not insane—not legally, that is, although he may have been medically insane.

At that point—February 10, 1903—Hooper offered to plead guilty to second-degree murder. The judge accepted, but refused to give Hooper the death penalty because of the likelihood of his medical insanity. Instead, the judge sentenced him to hard labor for the rest of his natural life in Sing Sing Prison in Ossining, New

York. Because he pled guilty, his motive was never revealed in court. Nor were his claims about a second man examined. Those bits of information eventually died with Hooper Young.

Hooper's conviction devastated John Willard, who initially believed his son was innocent of murder. He continued to live in the apartment and attended a branch of the Church there for the rest of his life.

Hooper's conviction also created a substantial burden for the members of the Church in New York City, who found themselves repeatedly having to defend the Church. In fact, public excitement was so high in the days immediately following Hooper's arrest that President McQuarrie said, "I am quite sure that if it had happened in a less populous city, or in one of the Southern states, none of us would have escaped lynching."12 Church members in New York responded mostly by living their lives as usual and referring policy questions to Church headquarters in Salt Lake, which in turn responded with occasional policy announcements.

As for Hooper Young's life behind bars, he was a model prisoner. If you think that "hard labor" consists of breaking up rocks with a pick axe like what's shown in those old grainy black-and-white movies, think again. Hooper spent most of his time working as a janitor in the prison chapel and perfecting his system of distilling water in the sun in the prison greenhouse.

In 1915, some Mormon missionaries showed up to visit Hooper in prison. The guard who escorted them described him as a bit flighty, even crazy. Hooper looked the missionaries in the eye, denied any responsibility for Anna Pulitzer's death, and blamed his vague faults on the "sins" of his parents. He tried to enlist them to get his father to intervene in his behalf. The missionaries left the prison that day feeling sorry for Hooper and wishing they could restore him to full fellowship in the Church.

In early 1924, before Hooper had quite served twenty years, he was released on parole into the custody of the Salvation Army. Conflicting stories exist as to what exactly happened between Hooper and his father in the time that followed, but apparently they reconciled: Hooper, by then insisting on being known as

"Billy," nursed his father during his final month of life and was by his side when he died of cancer in February at the age of seventy-nine.

You might think that's the end of what we know of Hooper Young. Well, not quite.

Historian Ardis E. Parshall, who has doggedly researched Hooper's trail following his father's death, has found most of the trail to be cold. There are, however, a couple of scintillating hints at where he might have gone and what he might have done.

In 1928, four years after his father's death, he was tramping around Fair Oaks, California, looking for one of his half-sisters.

In June 1937, a man named William Hooper Young submitted a Social Security claim on an account that listed his parents as John W. Young and Elizabeth Canfield. It seems that's our boy Hooper—the names of the parents were appropriate and so was the age: he would have been sixty-six.

But perhaps the most appalling hint of all is found in the records of Folsom Prison in Sacramento, California. On July 20, 1938, a prisoner named William Hooper Young was incarcerated in Folsom to begin a sentence of zero to fifteen years. His occupation was listed as salesman, and his record states he had formerly been incarcerated at Sing Sing in New York. *Sounds* like it could have been our boy, who by then would have been sixty-seven. His crime? Lewd acts with a minor, among other salacious offenses.

We don't know when and where William Hooper Young died. But those Folsom records do tell us one thing: after all that time, he must have still been struggling with those "carnal appetites."

Isaac Perry Decker, immortalized as the young boy holding his mother's hand and petting his dog on the bronze plaque at the This Is the Place Monument in Salt Lake City.

Isaac Perry Decker and the 1869 Measles Epidemic
Death and Dying Everywhere

Here's a news flash: medical knowledge has changed dramatically since 1869. So dramatically, in fact, that *lots* of people alive today have never even *seen* someone afflicted by the measles.

If you're one of them, here are the facts. There are two kinds of measles. The first, *rubeola* (sometimes called "red measles" or "hard measles"), is the most serious. It starts with fun-filled symptoms like fever, fatigue, cough, a runny nose, red eyes, and a loss of appetite. After a few days, here comes the rash: it starts on the face, spreads to the chest and back, and eventually the arms and legs. While it starts out as little red bumps, these eventually blend in with each other. Before long, you look red all over. Sort of like a bad sunburn. In fact, as it heals, the skin peels like it does with sunburn.

The measles themselves usually aren't what get you. It's the complications—most especially pneumonia. It's particularly dangerous in kids.

The other variety of measles is called *rubella* (or German measles), and is the less serious kind. It starts out the same as red measles, with the addition of swollen glands, but it's less likely to turn deadly. When the spots show up, they're usually more pink than red. In lots of cases, people don't even notice (or realize) they're infected. In some cases, though, swollen glands and aching joints might linger for as long as two weeks. The worst complication is when the measles are passed through the mother's blood to an unborn baby; the deleterious effects can include heart defects, hearing impairment, cataracts, learning disabilities, miscarriage, or stillbirth.

You might want to pay attention to those ads for vaccination.

Back in the day, of course, there was no vaccination against measles. You don't even have to go *that* far back: the vaccination wasn't introduced in the United States until 1963. The next year, the number of measles cases in the country fell from hundreds of thousands to tens of thousands—a number that dropped to mere thousands within twenty years.

As is obvious, our pioneer ancestors didn't have the vaccination against measles (or against anything else, for that matter). In their day, they got the bug and rode it out, hopefully to a satisfactory conclusion. Sadly, lots of them died in the epidemics that swept through every couple of years. One who was particularly affected by the measles epidemic of 1869 was Isaac Perry Decker, a fellow considered by some to be a bit of a rascal.

Isaac Perry Decker—known most of his life as Perry—was born as the "caboose" of his family on August 7, 1840, in Winchester, Illinois, to Isaac Decker and Harriet Page Wheeler. As it turns out, he became famous at a relatively young age—and you'll see why if you visit the bronze monument at the "This Is the Place" state park in Salt Lake City.

You see, Isaac Decker was one of the original pioneers in the vanguard company led across the plains in 1847 by his uncle, Brigham Young; he came to Utah with his mother and his stepfather, Lorenzo D. Young, who was one of the first to move out of their initial camp. (That stepfather was also the first to build a house outside the "Old Fort" when the pioneers arrived in Utah.) Isaac was one of three children from his family in that original band of pioneers; the others included his sister, Clarissa, and his slightly younger stepbrother, Lorenzo Sobieski Young. On July 24, 1847, Brigham Young hoisted himself up on one elbow from his sickbed in his wagon, proclaimed that the pioneer company was at the right place, and directed the wagons to drive on.

Memorialized on the bronze marker is Perry, who would turn seven in two weeks. He is holding on to his mother's hand but looking at his dog, who also made the journey. It was—and remains—his two minutes of fame.

But hold on. There *were* a couple of other incidents in Perry's life that resulted in a little renown. One was an episode that pretty much amounted to kidnapping, though we're the first to admit things were a lot different back in those days. And, when it comes right down to it, Perry might have actually been considered the hero in the situation.

Here's how it went down: Perry was in Kaysville, visiting his wife's sister, Ester Emily. Suddenly he heard a woman scream.[1] Following the screams, he entered the home and came upon a terrible scene: his sister-in-law was peering out of a wardrobe in dread fear as her husband, William Bosworth, was beating his two-and-a-half-year-old stepdaughter, Clara Latham. (Lots of steps and in-laws in this story.)

Perry immediately began fighting with Bosworth, and eventually got the better of him, knocking him to the floor. He then scooped little Clara into his arms and drew his line in the sand. The Bosworths were welcome to visit Clara any time they pleased, he said, but if they ever tried to claim her, Perry would beat Bosworth—to death this time.

Perry left the house, mounted his horse, and, the little girl in his arms, rode the twenty-five miles back home to Salt Lake City.

Imagine for a minute that you're Elizabeth Garratt Ogden, whom Perry had married on January 3, 1860, in Draper, Utah. Imagine, too, that you're minding your own business, getting supper ready. Then imagine how Elizabeth felt when Perry burst through the door, hot and dusty from his long ride, and thrust little Clara into her arms.

"Here is a child for you," he announced to her unceremoniously.

Life went on. Clara took the last name of Decker, remained with Perry and Elizabeth, and was loved as one of the family. She eventually married Thomas E. Browning, Ogden's chief of police.

More than anything, this episode speaks volumes about Perry. The fight that knocked William Bosworth to the floor must have been . . . well, pretty violent—violent enough to persuade Bosworth that he didn't want a rematch. After all, he never came around trying to get his stepdaughter back. That implies to us, reading between the lines, that Perry must have been both strong and intimidating. As a descendant penned, "I'm sure Perry was not a man to be taken lightly."[2]

There's not a lot written about Perry—and most of what *is* written was authored by descendants, both those who admired him and those who . . . well, didn't. One wrote that while Perry's older brother Charlie was "one of the greatest frontier heroes," Perry "was a spoiled child, a rascal, and a roustabout who drank a lot, rather neglected his remarkable wife . . . and their (at least eight) children, and spent his life in and out of trouble with the law." (Bring on the haters!)

Sadly, we're missing the salacious details about those repeated scrapes with the law. We do have just a taste from an article printed in the *Salt Lake Daily Tribune* on May 1, 1880, titled "The Stolen Horse." Right from the beginning it specifies that Perry Decker's trial for horse stealing "came off yesterday in the Police Court," and that Decker was discharged, since there was no evidence against him.

The article continues:

> [Perry] was furnished on the day of his arrest with a memorandum by one of the feeding stables of this city calling for two horses of a certain description. He went out to his range to hunt out the two animals and succeeded in getting only one, which, with a number of other horses, he was bringing to this city. [A man] met him and claimed one of the horses as his own, and Decker told him to take it then. It appears that the horse said to have been stolen is one which wandered off from the owner's herd

> some six months since, and had very naturally
> made a tour of the country about, prospect-
> ing it for a good vein of grass; that in his per-
> egrinations the equine mixed in with Decker's
> horses, thought to be a pretty fair set of steeds
> and thereafter abided with them. There was no
> evidence tending to criminate Mr. Decker in
> the transaction, and he was released.

We're assuming the story is true. If it isn't, it is certainly a creative one.

Isaac Perry Decker died January 24, 1916, in Provo, Utah, and was buried in Provo six days later. The opening sentence of that obituary hails him as one of the original band of pioneers who entered the Salt Lake Valley, and notes that the only remaining survivors of that band were W. C. A. Smoot of Salt Lake City and Perry's stepbrother, Lorenzo Sobieski Young. According to his obituary, Perry retained "a vivid recollection of those days [traveling to Utah] and often related experiences of the toilsome journey across the plains and the trials of pioneer life."

And there you have it. Except, of course, the part about the measles.

It was 1869, and the measles were once again sweeping into Utah. So many children were infected that doctors of the day declared it an epidemic. It was known as a "summer disease," and neither the doctors nor the parents knew how to prevent the spread of the highly contagious disease—or, for that matter, how to treat it.[3]

The *Deseret News* featured an article during the epidemic that blamed the disease on the fact that "the warm weather seems to have fairly set in, and as is usual in the summer season, there is considerable talk around of sickness among the children." The article goes on to name those sicknesses: cholera, scarlet fever, and measles. (As an aside, it mentioned that smallpox cases in California were on the decline.)

For parents like Perry and Elizabeth Decker, the advice for preventing the measles could not have been less effective. The article suggested washing vegetables, avoiding raw fruit, keeping homes and outhouses clean, bathing as necessary, and not allowing any standing water.

Those things *might* have helped in the prevention of cholera, but they had no bearing at all on the spread of measles, which was caused by a virus and which spread through human contact.

Perry and Elizabeth Decker, like all the other parents in Salt Lake City at the time, were watching their children like hawks, looking for the telltale signs and symptoms of the measles, most especially rash and fever. Some managed to escape. But most did not. And once the rash and fever developed, there was nothing parents or doctors could do to treat it.

Tragically, the same day the "helpful" article appeared in the *Deseret News*, Perry and Elizabeth Decker watched their three-year-old son, Edward, die from the measles. Even more tragically, he was not the first, but the third of their children to die. Edward was laid to rest in Brigham Young's cemetery in downtown Salt Lake City.

A week later, Edward's three-year-old cousin, Esther Ogden, also died of the measles and was buried with Edward. They were two of the fifteen children in Salt Lake City who succumbed to the measles that season. The youngest were infants; the oldest was nine.

The restored Toquerville LDS meetinghouse, still standing these many years later; it's now being used as the Toquerville City Hall.

ELI N. PACE
FORGET THE WHITES OF THEIR EYES—DON'T SHOOT BEFORE YOU AT LEAST KNOW WHO THEY ARE

REMEMBER JOHN D. LEE?

Sure you do. He's the guy who took the fall for the infamous Mountain Meadows Massacre, then was publicly executed for his crime in the town square in Beaver, Utah, and left lying in his open casket for a week afterward. Just so everyone got the message.

Well, this chapter isn't about him.

But it *is* about his son-in-law. And John D. Lee may be out of sight, but he actually figures prominently in the whole thing. In fact, you might even say he was the motive for it all.

Let us explain.

To make sense of this whole thing, we need to start with a daring river run—one that didn't even involve John D. Lee or his son-in-law, Eli N. Pace. It actually involved Major John Wesley Powell, an explorer, soldier, and scientist who is best known for his daring exploratory trips down the Colorado River in 1869 (when our story takes place) and 1872. In fact, he is credited with leading the first group of white men down the Colorado River and through the breathtaking gorge we now know as the Grand Canyon.

And it's those men—well, part of them, anyway—that figure prominently into our story.

Here's what happened: Powell was indeed on his way to that historic and groundbreaking Grand Canyon adventure with a handful of boats and a bigger handful of men. At this point, the ten-man expedition included Powell's mentally unstable but fiercely disciplined brother, Captain Walter Powell. It also included five "free-spirited" trappers who were along for the ride: Bill Dunn, Jack Sumner, Billie Hawkins, and brothers Seneca and Oramel Howell.

Things weren't going well on the river. As legendary Western historian Wallace Stegner pointed out in his biography of Powell, the major and his brother "represented military discipline and the officer class." The five trappers, on the other hand, "represented frontier independence and a violent distaste for discipline of any kind."[1] You know how they say traveling together brings out the worst in people? Well, this did exactly that.

As the men approached an immense and furious cataract that would later become known as Separation Canyon, three of the men—the Howell brothers and Bill Dunn—completely lost their nerve. The rapids were bad enough on their own, but recent rains had swollen the river and made them even fiercer. The three men didn't face exactly the best options: they could stay in the boat and attempt to survive the rapids, or they could try to scale the sheer canyon walls that surrounded them. They voted on the canyon walls and begged Powell to let them off the boat.

As it turned out, they weren't the first to cut ties and abandon the expedition when the going got really rough. And Powell wasn't the kind of guy to browbeat his expedition members into staying. So he let the men out. He was nice enough to leave an empty boat for them in case they found they weren't able to successfully scale the sheer cliffs.[2] Maybe once the river calmed down from the recent rains, he figured, the men might actually be able to make it down the river on their own.

And so it was that the three scrambled out of the boat, taking with them their provisions—including their packs, two rifles, a shotgun, a set of expedition papers, and a silver watch Jack Sumner asked them to deliver to his sister in case he drowned.[3] Guess it's always smart to hedge your bets. The three watched the rest of the expedition plunge into the vicious water and crash downstream, disappearing around the bend. (For inquiring minds who want to know, Powell and his remaining passengers did survive Separation Canyon and successfully completed their mission two days after separating from the three trappers.)

The hazards of the river might not have seemed too horrific after all when compared to the arduous climb the trappers now faced. It took them the better part of a day to scale the vertical walls of the Grand Canyon. Reaching the north rim, they set out across the Shivwits Plateau. After thirty miles of strenuous hiking, they climbed the gentle slopes of Mount Dellenbaugh, an extinct volcano. At its 6,990-foot summit, they took a breather while they got their bearings and planned what to do next. At least, that's what we *figure* happened, because—as you'll see in a minute—the three weren't heard from again after that day.

There are definite signs that the three—or Dunn, at least—were at the summit of Mount Dellenbaugh. In 1995 a hiker from Cedar City, Utah, found at the summit a small, badly tarnished brass plate that looked like it had once been fastened to the stock of a gun. Engraved on it in cursive writing was the name *William Dunn*.[4]

Back to our story. It seems the three took off from Mount Dellenbaugh and headed for the nearby Mormon settlement of Toquerville. As it turns out, staying in the boat even over horrific rapids would have *definitely* been better than that; you'll see why in a minute.

Seeing lights in one of the houses at Toquerville, the trappers knocked on the door and explained that they were seeking lodging for the night. Homeowner Richard Fryer was hesitant and relatively brusque. His wife was pregnant, and he didn't think it was such a good idea to take in three shabby-looking men under *those* sensitive circumstances. Nor could he just turn the men out into the dark, though. So he came up with an alternate plan: he threw on a jacket, grabbed his pistol, and led the three to his neighbor's house.

Enter Eli N. Pace. He answered the loud banging on his door only to see Richard Fryer and three scruffy strangers standing on his porch. Fryer identified the men as being from "the federal government"[5]—a case of mistaken identity if there ever was one—explained that they needed lodging for the night, and defended his decision to turn the men away based on his wife's delicate condition. Could Eli possibly take them in?

And here's where Eli N. Pace's intense paranoia settled in. He heard the words *federal government* and translated that into *federal agents*. And if anyone had reason to be suspicious of federal agents, it was Eli N. Pace. You see, he had recently been sealed to Nancy Lee, the daughter of John D. Lee. And his father-in-law, John D. Lee, had been evading federal agents for the twelve years since the Mountain Meadows Massacre, when 120 men, women, and children in the Baker-Fancher wagon train had been slaughtered. Lee had been on the run because he had been at Mountain Meadows.

Now Eli N. Pace stood face to face with three men he *thought* were federal agents. And he decided he had to act decisively "to protect Lee from three armed federal men coming out of nowhere."[6] Eli also wondered if the men were bounty hunters; after all, John D. Lee had a $5,000 reward on his head for anyone who could capture and turn him in. In those days, that was a *lot* of money.

Those three trappers couldn't have known what was coming—not based on Eli's composure, that is. He mumbled something about his situation being "similar" to Fryer's (was he hiding a pregnant wife in the closet?) and suggested they find the bishop and see if the three could bunk overnight at the ward house.

Here's where things get a little muddy. That bishop—Isaac C. Haight—had *also* been on the scene at Mountain Meadows. And for that same reason, he had *also* been eluding federal agents for the previous twelve years.

Like Fryer, Eli tossed on his jacket, picked up his pistol, and the five started walking toward the ward house. The three trappers didn't seem to be concerned that they were being escorted by two armed men—after all, they were strangers. And it was dark.[7]

As they approached the ward house, Eli volunteered to go get the bishop. He instructed Fryer to take the men to the ward house, where he indicated there should be some food and other supplies in the basement.

Eli then walked less than a block to the bishop's house and explained the situation to Isaac C. Haight. The blood drained out of the bishop's face as he collapsed into a chair. Ever since the day of the massacre at Mountain Meadows, he'd been living in constant fear that he would someday be implicated. Now there were three "federal agents" right in his own ward house, less than a block away. Had judgment finally come to Toquerville?

At that point, Eli had a decision to make. He could see the look of fear and desperation on his bishop's face. And he knew what this undoubtedly meant to his father-in-law. Wrapping his fingers around the handle of the pistol in his jacket pocket, he decided: it was time for him to defend his church and the people he loved.

Eli's thoughts raced.[8] He suggested that it would be best if the "agents" didn't see the bishop at all; the terrified bishop agreed. Eli then suggested that the bishop telegraph Church leadership in St. George—since they had recently gotten a spanky new telegraph machine—and ask for directions on what to do while Eli returned to the ward house. Cautioning Eli to be careful about what he and Fryer divulged to the agents, the bishop raced off to the telegraph office. Eli raced back to the ward house.

For the next two hours, telegraphs bounced back and forth between Bishop Isaac Haight and Apostle Erastus Snow, who was serving as president of the Southern Utah Mission (better known as "the cotton mission"). In the meantime, Fryer and Eli spent their time in the basement of the ward house, plying the three "agents" with food and drink. When Snow asked what the "agents" were up to, the bishop—undoubtedly fueled by panic and a healthy dose of his own paranoia—responded that they had gone straight to John D. Lee's son-in-law and their purpose was to investigate the Mountain Meadows Massacre.

Not true, and not true. But enough to rattle Apostle Snow.

Just think how the communication would have gone had it been someone other than the good bishop on the Toquerville end.

At the end of the two hours, the directive came from St. George: "A word to the wise should be sufficient."9

That missive didn't mention anything about murder . . . but unfortunately, that's how it was interpreted.

During those two hours in the basement of the ward house, Richard Fryer and Eli Pace had succeeded in gaining the trust of the three trappers. The trappers unloaded their firearms and stacked their guns on a shelf, right in front of the two Mormons. Simply put, they had no clue as to what was about to happen.

Two hours had elapsed, and the two Mormons figured they should have some direction from Church leadership by then. Richard left the ward house intent on learning if the bishop had been successful in alerting authorities. When he returned to the ward house and handed the final telegram to his buddy Eli Pace, things went down very quickly.

As author Wayne Atilio Capurro described it:

> With their guests seated at the basement table, they drew their handguns and fired point blank into the backs of the heads of Seneca Howell and William Dunn. . . . [T]he young Mormons fired their second volley into Oramel's heart.

> Before the sun rose the next morning, three of the first ten [white] men to navigate the Colorado through the Grand Canyon were buried deep beneath the earthen floor of the Toquerville Ward House [which, incidentally, still stands].10

Okay, *murder* was bad enough. But burying the bodies in the floor of the ward house? That's a whole new level of bad . . .

A few days later, Major John Wesley Powell himself came wandering through St. George, asking that local Saints keep a sharp eye out for the three missing trappers.11 With that, the pistol-happy Mormons at Toquerville discovered that they hadn't killed federal agents at all, but rather a trio of trappers who had bailed on an expedition through the Grand Canyon when the waters got too ferocious.

Oops.

Time to cover some back ends. The parties involved huddled and came up with a story they thought sounded plausible. And on September 7, 1869, an unidentified person anonymously sent a telegram to Apostle Snow in St. George. The telegram claimed that the three men had been killed by three Shivwits Indians. The Indians, the telegram said, were seeking revenge because the three trappers had earlier shot a squaw who was innocently gathering seed.[12] The telegram even claimed that the Shivwits had fed and watered the trappers before those same trappers so heinously killed the squaw. No wonder, it implied, the Shivwits were so furious.

Upon receiving the telegram, of course, Apostle Snow tracked down Major Powell and told him the sad news.

Powell was immediately skeptical about the Indian story. So was Jack Sumner, who had been a close friend of Dunn and the Howell brothers. Ironically, the night the three separated from the river expedition, the remaining men had sat around the campfire wondering what would happen to the three now that they were on their own. According to Sumner, everyone else in the expedition figured the Indians would find and kill the three trappers, but he adamantly disagreed:

> I had trained Dunn for two years in how to avoid a surprise, and I did not think the [Indians] would make open attack on three armed men. But I did have some misgiving that they would not escape the double-dyed white devils that infested that part of the country. Grapevine reports convinced me later that that was their fate.[13]

Sumner was referring, of course, to the Mormons in Southern Utah. He'd heard all about the Mountain Meadows Massacre and their continued insistence that it was *Indians* who had slaughtered the unfortunate Baker-Fancher party. So when he heard the Mormons in Toquerville insisting that Indians had killed his friends, he was immediately suspicious. This was sounding familiar.

Underscoring his suspicion was the fact that several years later during a drunken brawl, what should he see but the silver watch he had given Howell—you know, the one Howell was supposed to deliver to Sumner's sister in case he drowned. When he confronted the man about the watch, he gleefully boasted about how it had ended up in his hands. Sumner readily admitted that such was not conclusive evidence, but it was enough to convince him that "the Indians were not at the head of the murder, if they had anything to do with it."[14]

What happened a year later proves the old adage that truth is stranger than fiction. Because, you see, two different stories eventually emerged—one appearing to be a confession—about what happened to the three unfortunate trappers.[15]

In the first, Major John Powell, having cooled his heels in his hometown of Chicago for a year, decided to return to the Colorado River basin to explore some of its tributaries. Learning he was leaving for the area, some of the Howell family asked him to try to find out what happened to the brothers. Powell decided to enlist the help of Brigham Young, who volunteered his legendary Indian missionary, Jacob Hamblin. On September 5, 1870, the prophet accompanied Hamblin to meet Powell in Parowan with about forty Saints—among them, ironically, John D. Lee and another who had been on the scene at Mountain Meadows. They accompanied Powell as far as Pipe Springs, where Powell and Hamblin continued on alone across the Arizona Strip in the company of a handful of Kaibab Indians.

On September 19, just northeast of Mount Dellebaugh, the group met up with a contingency from the Shivwits who had allegedly shot Powell's men.

Astonishingly, the Shivwits owned up to the shooting.

They even provided details.

According to the Shivwit chief—with translation services provided by Hamblin—"We killed three white men." Okay, he didn't have their names, but the implication was strong enough. Another Shivwit filled in the color commentary: the three trappers had stumbled into the Shivwits' village, starving and fatigued. The Shivwits had fed them and allowed them to rest before sending them on their way.

Shortly after the trappers left, an Indian from across the Colorado showed up in the village and said that "a group of miners" had shot a squaw who was minding her own business and gathering seed. The Shivwits were furious, as is understandable. They set out to find the men and, upon discovering them, "surrounded the men in ambush, and filled them full of arrows."[16]

Of course, you and I know those bodies punctuated with arrows couldn't be our three trappers. After all, they were buried in the dirt floor of the ward house in Toquerville—filled with bullets, not arrows.

So much for *that* story—which, by the way, continued to be challenged for years.

In the second story, a grizzled old Colorado River guide named Otis "Dock" Marston swore on all that was good and right that he'd been told in confidence—by a *Mormon*, no less—that it was the Mormons who shot the three trappers.

Amazingly, Marston and all the others who claimed the Mormons were behind the dastardly deed were soundly dismissed by just about everyone—including renowned historian Wallace Stegner.

Until they found the letter.

Ninety-seven years after the murders—*ninety-seven years*— Wesley P. Larsen, a Mormon who had been the dean of the college of science at Southern Utah University in Cedar City, found a letter among a pile of debris in the bottom of an old trunk in Toquerville. The letter[17]—dated February 17, 1883—detailed that Dunn and the Howell brothers had been murdered in the Toquerville ward house by a pair of Mormons.

The never-before-published 1883 letter from William Leany Sr. to John Steele refers to "the day those three were murdered in our ward & the murderer killed to stop the shedding of more blood."[18]

There was some initial speculation about William Leany's soundness of mind, since he had earlier been beaten severely in the head and had sustained a skull fracture. (Ironically, he was beaten because he had sheltered and fed one of the suspected instigators of the Mountain Meadows Massacre. Apparently what goes around comes around.) But Leany was later considered to be of sound enough mind to make the allegation . . . and the rest is history.

He concluded his infamous letter with a clear declaration of his intentions: "But be assured that I will, God being my helper, clear my skirts of the mobbing, raking, stealing, whoredom, murder, suicide, infanticide, lying, slander & all wickedness & abominations."

Alrighty, then.

So what about Eli N. Pace? As we said, truth is stranger than fiction. On January 29, 1870—mere months after the murder of three men in the Toquerville ward house—Eli N. Pace was permanently silenced, shot through the heart.

At an inquest jury of three Mormons from Toquerville—one of whom was Bishop Isaac C. Haight—Pace's death was ruled a suicide.[19] When Pace's family challenged the inquest finding and asked for another review, the finding was the same.

But wait. Not everyone agreed with that. According to historian Michael Quinn, "Leany's letter . . . clearly indicated that the perpetrator [Mr. Pace] was killed to avoid retribution on the LDS community."[20]

And here's perhaps the most ribald theory of all: a letter written by John D. Lee's former neighbor that was published in the *Salt Lake Daily Tribune* on January 1, 1875, and signed only "Bosco" says it was—who else?—the wife.

That's right. Bosco wrote:

> [I]t is believed by many that he [Eli] got tired of her [Nancy] and was going to leave her. ONE NIGHT HE WAS KILLED, when no one but his wife was present. He was shot through the

heart, not with a shot-gun but with a Colt's revolver. His wife got a light, and then gave the alarm, stating that Eli had shot himself. A post mortem examination was held, but no evidence was brought to prove that Lee's daughter killed him.

However it happened, Eli N. Pace—who had committed murder in a Mormon ward house and buried his victims there—ended up dead himself not much later.

We don't know who did it. We'd just call it karma.

Julia Murdock Smith Dixon Middleton, the Prophet Joseph Smith's oldest surviving child and only daughter.

JULIA MURDOCK SMITH DIXON MIDDLETON
ADOPTED AT BIRTH AND IN DEATH

YOU PROBABLY ALREADY KNOW THE story of Julia Murdock and her twin brother being adopted at birth by Joseph and Emma Smith, who had lost their own prematurely born twins the same day. You probably also know about the tragic death of that twin brother during the persecution of the Prophet Joseph. You may even know that Julia was Joseph's oldest surviving child and only daughter.

But we're betting you don't know the colorful story of the rest of her life—or how she accumulated all those last names. One of Julia's biographers, Sunny McClellan Morton, sets the stage for Julia's colorful story with this tidbit:

> In some ways Julia remains an enigma, even to devotees of the prophet and his family—as if even after her death, she has been touched by the same disconnectedness that influenced her relationships and sense of self during her life. She was adopted: not quite a Smith, not quite a Murdock, and to historians of Mormonism, not quite a Mormon. Themes emerge: Julia's love and loyalty for those who claimed her as family, her conflicts of identity, and her deep sense of loss of her biologic genealogy.[1]

To begin, let's take a step back and look at Julia's birth parents, themselves interesting and colorful folk. Julia's birth father, John Murdock, was born July 15, 1792, in Kortwright, Delaware County, New York.[2] By the time he was twenty-seven, he left home, and three years later he was homesteading property in Orange Township, near Cleveland, Ohio. (That would make him thirty and still single—qualifying, according to Brigham Young, as a menace to society.)

Julia's birth mother, Julia Clapp—for whom our Julia was named—was born February 23, 1796, in Warrensville, Ohio. While John Murdock's family boasted nothing to make headlines, Julia came from a prominent family: her mother came to the area in 1806 as one of the first female settlers, and her father was a renowned judge. Oh, well, you know what they say: opposites attract.

We don't know how John and Julia met or anything about their courtship, but they married on December 14, 1823, in a ceremony conducted by Julia's uncle, who was a justice of the peace. They immediately settled into life as a married couple on their thirty-five-acre homestead in Orange Township and began building their family. Orrice was born a year after their marriage, and John Riggs and Phebe followed in 1825 and 1828. In 1829, they buried an unnamed infant. Soon after, they purchased more land to support their growing family.

In November 1830, life as they knew it changed for the Murdocks when Mormon missionaries arrived in northeast Ohio, preaching the restored gospel. The Murdock family turned out to be particularly receptive to their message. John stayed up all one night reading the Book of Mormon; abandoning his former faith, the Disciples of Christ, he was baptized the next day, November 5, 1830.

Emerging from the waters of baptism, he took the Book of Mormon home and read the entire thing to Julia. She was as convinced as he of its truth, and was baptized nine days later.

Sadly, their acceptance of the gospel and baptism into the Church drove a serious wedge between them and Julia's family.

Filled with enthusiasm for his new faith, John paid a visit to the Clapps and preached the gospel to Julia's parents. Members of the Disciples of Christ, they were, as he wrote in his journal, "very unbelieving and hard."[3] Their bitterness toward the Church was so intense, in fact, that though the "greatest friendship" existed between the two families before the Murdocks joined the Church, the Clapps completely cut off the Murdocks—including their own daughter—once they were baptized.

The Clapps weren't the only people with whom John Murdock shared the gospel. Almost immediately after his own baptism, he started traveling throughout the countryside as a Mormon missionary. He quickly built up a local congregation of about eighty people.

Soon he found he no longer had time to tend to his property *and* fulfill his missionary responsibilities, so in February 1831 he yanked up his family by the roots and moved them in with friends Caleb and Nancy Baldwin. The Baldwins, also Mormon converts, lived fewer than three miles from the Murdocks. With that move, John no longer had the pressure of land to take care of. From that time forward, he devoted his full time to preaching the gospel.

John was thrilled with the new arrangement, but we have to wonder about poor Julia. Things must have been a bit tough for her. For one thing, she was seven months pregnant—with *twins*. For another, her husband was always gone. And don't forget: she was completely estranged from her family as a result of embracing the gospel. What it all boiled down to was this: she was heavy with child—make that two children—and trying to care for three small children completely on her own, all in a neighbor's home. Things couldn't have been easy.

On April 30, 1831, Julia gave birth to twins Joseph and Julia. John, who was out preaching that day, *barely* made it back in time for the delivery.

Six hours later, Julia died.

What on earth happened? The only clue we have was in John's journal entry:

The children were born without any great agony
or pain to the Mother, and all appeared to be
doing well, except the after-birth was not taken
away, yet there was no suspition [*sic*] of death or
danger. I had just at this time went to the door
to speak to some person when she sent for me
to come in. Immediately I went to her bed. She
appeared to look fresh and be doing well, but she
told me she was going, and reached out her hand
and shook hands with me and every person in
the room and bid us farewell, and immediately
folded her hands across her own stomach, shut
her eyes, and went to sleep in Jesus.[4]

There was John, a widower, left with five young children to
care for—including newborn twins. He had also recently accepted
a new full-time missionary assignment and knew he needed to
leave. What to do?

Julia's parents, the Clapps, lived nearby and could have
provided well for the children. But that wasn't an option for
John—not only had they completely estranged themselves from
the Murdocks, but John knew his children would not be given *any*
religious training in the Mormon Church. Quite the contrary, in
fact; they would have been alienated against the Church. Because
of that, he temporarily turned his three oldest children over to
local Mormon families who agreed to care for them while he
served his mission.

But what about the twins? Keep in mind this was in a day
before readily available infant formula and disposable diapers (or,
for that matter, any commercially manufactured diapers at all),
and little if any support for single fathers. John was facing a real
dilemma.

He knew the twins needed constant care and a wet nurse—a
role into not just anyone could step. But John knew someone who
could be exactly that. Just that day, Joseph and Emma Smith had
welcomed premature twins, who had died at birth. He arrived at

the Smith home and offered the twins to the grieving couple—not just for the period while he was on his mission, but permanently.

Years later, Julia took her father to task for what he did, writing that if her mother "has seen the way her family have been divided and estranged she must feel unhappy." In response, John defended his actions by explaining that he had been left with five small children. As he wondered what to do with them, he wrote, "is it duty to place them in the hands of those who oppose . . . the authority of God . . . (for this is what your mother's relatives did) or shall I place them where they can be taught in the faith and principles of salvation?"[5] You have to admit, he makes a good argument.

Interestingly, John changed his story a bit—okay, *quite* a bit—three decades later when Julia once again challenged him about his decision. This time, he made it sound like the Smiths were the instigators, coming to him and begging for the babies. He also explained away his subsequent absence from Julia's life by saying the *Smiths* had set up strict guidelines about the terms of the adoption:

> Brother Joseph, hearing of the death of my wife and the two children left, sent word to me that he would take the children and raise them, and also sent a man and woman for them, and I sent them to him. He then lived in Kirtland and when I afterwards went to Kirtland Sister Smith requested me not to make myself known to the children as being their father. It was a hard request and I said but little on the subject. She wanted to bring the children up as her own and never have them know anything to the contrary, that they might be perfectly happy with her as their Mother. This was a good thought, yet selfish, and I was sensible it could not always remain so. Joseph told me it would one day all come to light, which it appears has taken place

without my divulging it, for I have always held
my peace. . . . I resolved to wait till time and
providence should divulge the matter.[6]

John seemed not only surprised, but unhappy about those terms. He strongly implied that had Emma not insisted on such conditions, he would have pursued an open relationship with Julia. Apparently Emma's terms came as a bit of a surprise to Joseph Smith as well. The two men ended up talking it over and consoling themselves with the belief that things would ease up a bit as time went on, which was pretty much how adoptions went back then.

When it comes right down to it, things were a bit muddy for John. It was clear that though he was completely out of the picture as far as Emma Smith was concerned, John still considered himself the father of the twins. As just one piece of evidence of that, he continued to financially support them even after placing them with the Smiths.[7] As for Julia, once she learned that she was adopted, she was pretty much forced to abide by Emma's conditions, which meant she was not allowed to identify herself with the Murdock family—that in the midst of a society that didn't really allow her to be a Smith, either. And while John may have drifted in and out of the picture throughout Julia's life, there is no question that Julia loved and accepted Emma as the only mother she ever knew, always calling her *mother*. In fact, the only time she intimated otherwise was later in her life—when writing to members of her birth family, she always called Emma her "foster mother."[8]

Julia also showed great affection for the Smiths' other children, her adoptive brothers. She signed one letter to Joseph III—to whom she was particularly close—"with much love I am always your sister." And she expressed especially great maternal love for her youngest brother, David Hyrum, whom she helped to raise.[9]

But hold on just a minute: in all her interactions with the Smiths, Julia seemed totally integrated into the family. However, her letters to the Murdocks later in her life, beginning when she was about seventeen, paint a different picture: one of "security and loss, conflicting loyalties and desires—a story that shows that although she did her best to be a Smith, she knew she didn't belong with them."[10]

To figure out why Julia was tossed into such a difficult situation, it's important that we realize that adoption in the 1830s was a far cry from the legal and social institution we know today.[11] In fact, the law never got involved at all in adoptions; a child was simply placed in an adoptive home through family or friends. Most of the time, an adopted child grew up in a town where everyone knew the story of her birth and adoption—and that was certainly the case with Julia. In fact, Julia's "town"—a tightly knit group of Mormon converts—moved along with her and the Smith family as they moved from Kirtland to Missouri to Nauvoo. That group of converts, of course, included her birth father, who made those treks along with the rest of the Saints.

Let's face it: though Emma wanted to keep the adoption a big secret, Julia never really got away from the folks who had witnessed her adoption firsthand. John was scarcely the only person in Julia's life who could have pulled her aside and spilled the beans.

And there's more about adoption in that day of which we should be aware:

During the early 1800s, adoption was viewed as a benevolent act on the part of the adoptive parents rather than as fulfillment of a couple's desire to become parents. Relationships with birthparents sometimes continued, and adoptive families often filled a fostering or surrogate role rather than that of full-fledged replacement parents. Adoptive mothers like Emma were not necessarily considered "real moms" because they hadn't given birth to the adoptive child. Therefore, society would have considered Julia to be a part of the Smith household but not a real "Smith child" like her Smith brothers. She would still have been a Murdock, especially since her father lived nearby, and it would normally have been acceptable for some sort of relationship to continue between Julia and her father.[12]

And so we see that there was nothing cut-and-dried or uncomplicated about Julia's adoption—and plenty that could have left her a bit unhinged.

The whole thing also raises another interesting point. Since there was absolutely no legal involvement in the adoption, couldn't John have come back and claimed the twins once he remarried? Legally, he certainly could have. But there was another factor at work: John himself had experienced an extremely unhappy childhood at the hands of an abusive stepmother. The *last* thing he wanted for his own children was a stepmother, if he could help it. He knew he would likely remarry, and he wrote in his journal about the concern it caused him: "[I] decreed in my heart, that a second wife in my house, should never tyrannize over a first woman's children."

John *did* remarry—five more times. Five years following Julia Clapp Murdock's death, he married a woman who died not long after in Far West, Missouri. A third wife died in Nauvoo. Seems like John Murdock wasn't having the best of luck when it came to holy matrimony. Finally, he struck gold in the longevity department in March 1846 when he married his fourth wife, Sarah Zufelt Weire. Not sure what happened to her or when, but his fifth marriage ended in divorce in 1859. At that point, he apparently called it quits as far as marriage was concerned.

While Julia stayed put in Nauvoo (more about that in a few minutes), John and Sarah left Nauvoo in 1847 and made the trek to Salt Lake City under the leadership of Brigham Young. They took with them three children: Gideon, a son from John's third marriage; George Weire, Sarah's six-year-old son from her previous marriage; and Mary Cooper, a two-year-old foster daughter (not sure what the story was there).

What about John's children from his first marriage—Julia's birth siblings? John eventually reclaimed them (more about that in a minute, too). We do know that Orrice and John Riggs, ages twenty-two and twenty-one at the time, went west with the Mormon Battalion.

Now you know a little about the Murdock family and how adoption worked in the 1830s. Let's go back to the story of the infant twins who got adopted by the Smiths. . . .

Joseph and Emma initially lived with their newborn twins in a cabin on the Isaac Morley farm in Kirtland. As the twins were close to turning six months old in mid-September 1831, the Smiths moved in with John and Alice Johnson in nearby Hiram, Ohio. As you'll undoubtedly recall, it was one in a series of many moves the Prophet was forced to make with his young family.

In late March 1832, eleven-month-old Joseph contracted the measles—a critically serious disease in those days. Hoping Julia wouldn't also be infected, Emma decided the babies should sleep in separate rooms. And that's how it happened that Joseph Smith was sleeping with Joseph in the front room of the house while Emma was sleeping with Julia in a separate room. Little could Emma have known that Julia was already in the early stages of the infection though she had not yet manifest the characteristic rash. In other words, both twins were sick.

And that's when tragedy hit.

No, not the measles . . . well, not exactly. During the middle of the night, a mob broke into the Johnson home where Joseph was sleeping with his baby boy in the front room. The mob dragged Joseph out into the frigid air and tarred and feathered him. In the chaos that ensued, both twins were exposed to the night air. Five days later, young Joseph died from his infection as a result of the exposure.

And what an irony: many of the mob members that night were members of the Disciples of Christ. You remember them: Julia Clapp's family remained steadfast members of the faith. As one biographer wrote of the mob that descended that chilly March night, "though none of the rabble were Clapps, the irony remains that members of the Disciples church may have indirectly contributed to the death of the Clapp grandchild."[13] Egads.

In June of that same year, John Murdock returned from his missionary labors and was understandably saddened to learn that baby Joseph had died. He was, however, glad to see that Julia was still doing well with the Prophet and his family—and he confirmed his earlier decision to leave her there. He did make the rounds, however, to gather up his older children, paying full price to the guardians who had cared for them. The three had stayed in three separate homes during John's absence.

John Murdock didn't have much time to cool his heels and get reacquainted with his children. On August 29—less than three months later—Joseph Smith called John on another mission in a revelation that specified "thou art called to go into the eastern countries from house to house, from village to village, and from city to city, to proclaim mine everlasting gospel unto the inhabitants thereof, in the midst of persecution and wickedness" (D&C 99:1).

You can read the whole thing in section 99. This was no short-term mission call; in verse 8, the Lord tells John "thou shalt continue proclaiming my gospel until thou be taken." Yikes. Remember that John had just gathered up his oldest three children a few months earlier—and the Lord provided an important caveat in the revelation: "it is not expedient that you should go until your children are provided for, and sent up kindly unto the bishop of Zion" (v. 6).

If John was anything, he was completely obedient. He responded:

> "[I] accordingly sent my three oldest children to Bishop Partridge . . . with some money for their support. . . . I disposed of my property and gave some to Bro. Joseph, sent some to the Bishop in Mo. for the support of my children. . . . And now I was prepared to travel and preach the gospel without being cumbered with either family or property."[14]

Julia, of course, stayed with the Smith family, as John hadn't been "cumbered" with her for quite some time. And things in Julia's life were going along great until, at the tender age of five, she found out she was adopted—and it wasn't pretty. As we mentioned, Julia was never far from a whole gaggle of people who knew the entire story of her birth and adoption, and they all knew enough to keep their mouths shut. But there *were* a few newcomers in town, and, well, you know how ugly gossip can get.

Sadly, the Smiths were not exempt from the gossip mill. In fact, they were often right in the middle of it. And the gossips went to town with the fact that Julia was in the Smith home. Maybe as a result of unfounded rumors that were circulating about exactly where Julia had come from, one of the neighbors finally yanked five-year-old Julia aside and broke the news of her adoption to her just about as insensitively as possible.

The revelation of being adopted can be tough on anyone. One psychologist wrote, "Hearing that one was not born to one's mother is a profound and unrecognized trauma. . . . The child finds it incomprehensible." She did add, however, "That is not to say that the child is irreparably damaged."[15]

Years later, Julia wrote to her birth brother, John Riggs Murdock:

> Mine has been no easy life. Until I was a child
> of five years old I was happy, it was then I was
> first told I was not a Smith, and by Mrs. Walk-
> er, she was little older than myself, and she
> done it through spite. . . . From that hour I was
> changed. I was bitter even as a child. O how it
> stung me when persons have inquired, "Is that
> your adopted daughter?" of my foster mother
> [Emma]. John, you little know what I suffered
> in my early life, and even since I was grown.[16]

How dreadfully tragic to be bitter, even as a child.

In the same letter, she asked her brother a question she would later ask John Murdock: "Why was it . . . that I could not have been raised with my own blood and kin and not with strangers, and bear a name I had no claim on?" Julia's reaction here would seem to be normal to anyone who learns she is adopted—but it doesn't mesh with the way she referred to the Smith family so often, even during her later years.

Subsequent statements in that same letter point out her obvious mixed emotions:

> "I shunned you and my father [the Murdocks],
> and why? Because I had a dread of being tak-
> en from those I was raised with and loved [the

Smiths], with the same love that should have been yours. Many a sleepless night I have spent thinking of this when I was child. But I was a woman in thought, even then. After seeing some of you [the Murdocks], I have almost cursed the day I was born. . . . I chose to love those I knew."[17]

The conflict that seems to have raced in her mind, "even then," must have been sheer torture.

The revelation of her adoption was only one of the factors that led to Julia's unhappy childhood, as she would remember it. There were constant upheavals as the Smiths were forced to move from one place to another, rarely having a spot to call their own. They often took in either boarders or refugees, something that would have complicated matters, to say the least. And face it: as much as we love and revere the Prophet, it had to be a bit tough to have an adopted father who was both venerated and hated for his religious beliefs, not to mention being gone much of the time.

And that's not all: More children were subsequently added to the family. Though Julia seemed to have a close, loving relationship with them, she likely would have been expected to take on at least some child-care and household responsibilities as a result. Following Julia's adoption, the Smiths added six sons: Joseph III (born in 1832, when Julia was just one), Frederick (1836), Alexander (1838), Don Carlos (born in 1840, living just more than a year), an infant son who died at birth in 1842, and David Hyrum (who was born in 1844, five months after the Prophet was martyred).

Julia's relationship with her father is a bit difficult to sort out. She was barely more than a child when he was killed, so she never knew him as an adult. Letters between Joseph and Emma indicate that Julia adored him as a child and missed him terribly during the periods he was away from home. As for Joseph, he clearly doted on Julia, calling her "a lovely little girl" and proclaiming his love for her in the written word. Later in her life, it's entirely possible that she developed some indecisive feelings toward him as she reflected on his religious faith, something that caused not only his premature death but, as she saw it, significant suffering for both her and Emma. Her relationship with Emma, on the other hand, was "the most solid and rewarding that she seems to have had."[18]

Julia's formal education started in Kirtland, when Eliza R. Snow moved in and taught both six-year-old Julia and five-year-old Joseph III. For the first year the family lived in Nauvoo, there was no organized school—so Emma took over in a homeschooling arrangement common in the American frontier, teaching Julia how to cook, sew, and read.

The rest of Julia's childhood and youth were spent in Nauvoo, where the family shuttled from a crowded log home on the banks of the Mississippi River to the Mansion House, a combination home and hotel where the family was living at the time of the martyrdom.

During her childhood, Julia was a popular girl who had many friends. Things became much more sober for Julia when she was twelve: two of her baby brothers died within a few months of each other. During that time, she sat for a watercolor portrait painted by Sutcliffe Maudsley; though the original painting has been lost, a black-and-white photo of it still exists. A description of that portrait provides an early narrative of what Julia looked like as a child moving into young adulthood:

> [Julia] dressed for her portrait in black silk for mourning and holds the grief symbol, a large handkerchief. Instead of white sleeves from elbow to wrist, she has more black silk. This amount of black indicated that Julia is taking on adult mourning practices. Only white cuffs and white lace at the neck relieve the shade. Her hairstyle elaborately uses all her long hair, with front braids looping below her ears and ringlets on the neck, with many braids coiled in a bob.

The black-and-white photo of the watercolor shows prominent features—thick hair, large eyes, and a forceful mouth—that remained throughout her life.

The very next year, when Julia was thirteen, the Prophet Joseph Smith was murdered at Carthage in an act of mob violence. As you might well imagine, Julia's life changed dramatically as a result, and not just because her father was gone. Most of Julia's friends fairly soon evacuated the city and set out for the Rocky Mountains, while Emma chose to stay in Nauvoo—with all her children tucked securely under her wing. And that's not all: Though Julia had not yet formed a relationship with her birth father, John Murdock, she knew who he was. And she also knew he took his family and left Nauvoo with the rest of the Saints. And there, she undoubtedly felt, went any chance of getting to know him.

Even though almost all the Mormons had cleared out of Nauvoo, the anti-Mormon sentiment—and accompanying agitation—was still severe, so Emma decided to take her kids and get out of Dodge, so to speak. In the winter of 1846, they moved 150 miles up the Mississippi River from Nauvoo to Fulton City, Illinois, a small village of about four hundred people. Joseph Smith III described it as a swampy prairie wilderness with grass growing six feet tall wherever the ground was damp. He also remembered a bunch of the youth from Fulton City—including Julia, it can legitimately be assumed—riding in a sleigh eighteen miles down the road to a larger town (that wouldn't take much!), when they enjoyed suppers and dances.

Julia's life underwent another fairly dramatic change on December 23, 1847, when Emma Smith married non-Mormon Major Lewis C. Bidamon. At the age of sixteen and in the snap of a finger, Julia gained not only a stepfather but three younger stepsisters. There's no evidence that Julia and her stepfather had a negative relationship; in fact, since Julia left home two years later, he probably didn't have much influence on her as a father at all. The Smith/Bidamon gang moved back to Nauvoo, where Lewis built Emma a large brick house.

In 1849, when she was eighteen, Julia met and married Elisha Dixon, the first of her two husbands. It seems to have happened pretty quickly and without much input or any approval from her mother. As Joseph III described it:

> [A] slender, blue-eyed, fairskinned, light-haired fellow came to town. He was a magician by profession, a most successful prestidigitator, who had been traveling about as a gypsy king. He had become ill and found it necessary to stop at Nauvoo to recuperate, boarding meanwhile at our house along with a friend named Charles Pease. Before the winter was over he had fallen in love with my sister Julia and married her. She was of age and, of course, her own mistress, and though the man was practically a stranger to us, Mother did not feel she could assert any authority to prevent her making the alliance. Besides, he seemed honest enough, and of pleasant disposition.

Oh, boy—your only daughter marries a *prestidigitator*? And a gypsy king at that? You can bet Emma didn't feel she could exercise any authority over Julia to actually *stop* the marriage, but can you just imagine how she must have felt? In the first place, he was twice Julia's age, she being eighteen and he thirty-six. That's not all: he hailed from Mechanicsburg, New York, and Emma knew nothing about his family, something that undoubtedly made her nervous. Then there was his physical stature: he was a little slip of a man who suffered from a plethora of health problems. (Julia, who was tall, hale, and hearty, once exulted that he had finally gained enough weight to tip the scales at 135 pounds.)

At first blush, it doesn't really seem to be a match made in heaven.

The marriage certainly had its share of ups and downs, and Julia often found herself alone. Right after they were married, Elisha—undoubtedly responding to some pressure from his mother-in-law—abandoned prestidigitation and got a job in St. Louis that paid a whopping forty dollars a month. But only a few months later, he was back in Nauvoo: when a cholera epidemic broke out in St. Louis, he turned tail and ran.

Just as well that he was back in Nauvoo. Emma no longer had the strength and stamina to run the Mansion House, so she turned the management of it over to Elisha for a year. It had to have been a nerve-wracking decision, but she was pleasantly surprised when he made a number of sorely needed improvements to the hotel.

Her elation may have been premature: at the end of that year, Elisha's health nosedived—in fact, it flat-out failed—and his doctor told him he needed to go south to a warmer climate. Okay, south is one thing. Elisha decided to go *way* south, setting out alone in December 1849 for Cuba. Yup, that's south, all right.

He never made it to Cuba. He made it only as far as St. Louis, when his health became too bad to go on. He came crawling back to Nauvoo, his tail between his legs, sometime in early 1850. The census for that year lists him living in Nauvoo and working as a tailor. For the next two years, he and Julia once again ran the Mansion House.

In the spring of 1852, Elisha finally made it "south" when he and Julia relocated to Galveston, Texas. At least this time he took Julia with him. Working out of Galveston, Elisha tended bar on a river boat. He was often gone, sometimes for as long as two weeks at a time, mixing drinks for the passengers on the boat. It was a time of frequent loneliness for Julia.

While she may have been lonesome for her husband, she seems to have loved Galveston. In a letter written on March 25, 1852, she enthused about her four pets—three birds and a dog. Her portrayal of the area was blissfully enthusiastic, describing warm days; cool, beautiful moonlit nights; breezes that fan the brow with perfumes drifting from orange and lemon groves; and a gulf that lulls one to sleep. While expressing fear of hurricanes, she ridiculed the astonishment of Texans experiencing their first snow: "Why does it fall in flakes, says one, as though it would fall in chunks. It made me laugh"[19] (spelling corrected).

As the summer of 1853 approached, Julia decided it was nigh time she meet her in-laws, so she planned a trip to Mechanicsburg, New York. But that, just like Elisha's planned trip to Cuba, was not to be. In May 1853, the boiler on Elisha's boat exploded; he was severely burned when he was thrown into the ash pan. After three weeks of fighting for his life, Elisha died.

Elisha's friend Charles Pease—you remember, the other magician who had arrived in Nauvoo with Elisha—was also badly burned "and greatly shattered in the nerves." Julia, who already knew Charles well, took him to Nauvoo and tried to nurse him back to health. Despite her efforts, Charles died within a few weeks.

Julia went to her home in Galveston and packed up her goods, hopped on the first train out of Galveston, and returned to Nauvoo, a twenty-two-year-old, childless widow. She moved back in with Emma. Those around her were surprised at how quickly she recovered from her husband's death and plunged back into Nauvoo's social scene. (Okay, no snickers here.) In a letter to Joseph III not quite two years later, she described herself as "wild as a March hare!"[20]

Later that summer, in July 1855, Julia boldly signed up for a river trip over rough waters that her friends were too timid to attempt. But not Julia—she went for it with all pistons firing, despite the hazards, and reported afterward that she had a delightful time.

Part of her delight may have centered in one of the other passengers—an Irish Catholic named John Jackson Middleton, five years her senior. Emma may have been disturbed over Elisha Dixon's family background (or lack thereof), but John seemed solid: the Middletons, original settlers of Nauvoo, were prominent merchants in town and were counted among the most socially elite. Now *this* was more like it.

John and Julia married the next fall, on November 19, 1856— three years, give or take, from the time her first husband died. Just shy of one year after their wedding—on November 9, 1857— Julia was baptized into the Catholic Church. It seems that John was not only a Catholic, but was strongly opposed to anything Mormon. In fact, he once tried to persuade Joseph III to abandon the RLDS Church (the Reorganized Church of Jesus Christ of Latter Day Saints, of which he eventually became president). For that and other reasons, Joseph III adamantly disliked John for the rest of his life.

Apparently Emma was so busy worrying about John's family background that she didn't worry much about *him*, and you'd better believe there were some problems there. For starters, he was an alcoholic, something that had prevented him from becoming a priest as he had originally planned. He was chronically ill, no doubt in part because of the alcohol. And he never really stuck with anything for long. Early in their marriage, John and Julia bought a small farm on the shores of the Mississippi River just two miles south of Nauvoo, but John quickly tired of farming. Then he took up being a lawyer, but his alcoholism rapidly got in the way of that.

Finally, the two sold their forty-acre farm. Julia also sold the city lot she owned. The two moved to St. Louis with $5,000 in their pocket, at least half of which belonged to Julia. There they bought a home on Chestnut Street, and John went to work first at an iron company, then at a pork processing company. Until he lost interest, that is.

Joseph III, Julia's devoted brother, visited the Middletons in St. Louis and didn't have much good to say about his sister's husband. He later described his brother-in-law as "the most outrageous slave to his appetites I ever saw; lazy and vicious in an extreme. An Irishman of lordly pretentions."[21] Joseph III didn't stop there. He also said that John's drinking was so heavy that it had estranged him from his own family, caused violent acts against his own father, and resulted in repeated attempts to borrow money from various family members. Emma Smith also wrote disparagingly about John and, on a number of occasions, about Julia's "trying life."

As for Julia's birth brother, John Riggs Murdock, he said— without elaborating—that Julia "had been very unfortunate in her second marriage."[22] Try reading between the lines on that one.

Joseph III needn't have worried about his sister being with such a cad for much longer. In 1877, John simply deserted Julia, taking off for New Mexico as a vagabond. Julia realized her marriage was over and returned penniless to Nauvoo and her mother. She had nothing but the clothes on her back and a feather bed.

Julia moved in to the Riverside Mansion, the brick home Lewis Bidamon had built, where she lived with Emma and Lewis. The two women lovingly cared for each other: Julia was suffering from painful sores on several parts of her body, and Emma's health was rapidly failing. Julia, Joseph III, and Alexander Smith were at Emma's side when she died on April 30, 1879.

Julia was named in Emma's obituary as one of her children who mourned her passing. But even then there was the "separation"— the obituary pointedly distinguished that Julia was *adopted*. Even in her mourning, the label was in her face.

The end seemed to be drawing near for Julia. She was widowed, abandoned, childless, alone, and had just lost the most solid relationship in her life—her mother. With no assets of her own, she returned to Andover, Missouri, with her brother Alexander; she lived with him for a short time before moving in with James and Samantha Moffitt—prosperous Catholics who were friends of the Middletons and known for "taking in strays."

If you think it's strange that Julia was still trading in on her status as John Middleton's wife, think again—they had never gotten a divorce. In fact, her obituary starts out with the fact that she is "wife of John Middleton."[23]

By this time Julia had cancer in her right breast. Joseph III visited his sister while she was living with the Moffitts and claimed that the cancer was due to a "severe blow" she had suffered,[24] stopping just shy of saying that the violent and alcoholic John Middleton had inflicted that blow during one of his drunken rages. There were periodic hints that Julia had suffered physical abuse, but nothing direct was ever said or written. Before leaving, Joseph III gave James and Samantha enough money to cover Julia's care and to pay for burial expenses and a headstone.

Regardless of the cause of her cancer, her circumstances in the Moffitt home were ideal for her. It was a large frame house situated at the top of a hill and surrounded by peaceful meadows and forests. Both James and Samantha rendered patient and tender care to her until she died September 10, 1880, at the age of forty-nine, shortly after Joseph III returned home from visiting her.

Julia was laid to rest in the Moffitt family plot in St. Peter and Paul's Cemetery—the Catholic section of the Nauvoo Cemetery, located on a gently winding road at the edge of town. The location of her grave indicates the close relationship James and Samantha developed with her in the short time she lived with them: she is buried immediately behind their joint grave, a space that is usually reserved for children.

Her obituary, which appeared in the *Nauvoo Independent* on September 17, 1880, starts with—what else?—the story surrounding her adoption. Even in death, she couldn't escape the thing that had apparently caused her such distress.

The obituary is colorful in itself. In describing her first marriage, it specified that "at the age of seventeen [she was] engaged to marry a man named Dixon, which met the objection of her foster-mother—Mr. Smith having been killed before that time. But as in most of other cases, where love yields not to dictation, she left home and married the man of her choice. But after a few years she was compelled to wear the weeds of widowhood. . . ."

Weeds?

The obituary concludes:

> Mrs. Middleton was a woman of the most exemplary character—an advocate of all the graces and virtues and had a strong loving disposition for her friends which firmly endeared her to them. She was considerably above the medium of intelligence and of an indomitable

spirit which fully manifested itself in the trying ordeal of sickness through which she passed
before the severance of the link which bound
her to this earthly sphere. Although she knew
that death was fast approaching she remained
cheerful and resigned. She leaves many friends
who deeply regret her death.

Before leaving the story of Julia Murdock Smith Dixon
Middleton, we should mention one peculiar thing. Throughout
her life, it is obvious that Julia was surrounded—and
influenced—by men of powerful religious persuasion. First, of
course, was her father, the Prophet who restored the gospel to the
earth, a man who was martyred for his faith. Then there was her
favorite and beloved brother, Joseph III, who eventually became
the president of the RLDS Church. And finally, of course, there
was her staunchly Catholic husband, John Middleton. Despite
that—and, who knows, maybe *because* of it—religion never
seemed to be particularly important to Julia. Her vast collection
of letters never debated religious subjects at all, and when she did
use any religious language, it was strictly nondenominational.[25]

Well, that's about it—except for one more colorful detail.[160]
Julia was adopted in life, but she was also adopted in death. On
December 16, 1884, in the St. George Temple—four years after
her death—Julia Smith Murdock Dixon Middleton was baptized
by proxy into the LDS Church in the St. George Temple. Two
days later, she was endowed by proxy in the same temple.

And then, on December 19 and in the same temple, she and
the entire Murdock family were "spiritually adopted" into the
Hyrum Smith family, a practice that was common before 1894.
And so it was that she was adopted again.

Let's hope *this* adoption is nothing but a source of great joy
to her.

When Andrew Balfour Hepburn couldn't get inside the building to assault James Marsden, he simply smashed his fist through the window.

ANDREW BALFOUR HEPBURN
AND JAMES MARSDEN
A HOODLUM AND A STAKE PRESIDENT GO HEAD TO HEAD

IN JUNE 2013, HISTORIAN ARIS E. Parshall gave a paper at the Mormon History Association that had people rolling in the aisles. It focused on a "disturbance" in a chapel in England, and as part of the larger picture, it also zoomed in on nineteenth-century British "hooliganism" as related to the Latter-day Saints.

She followed her presentation up a week later by publishing her paper on her blog.[1] If you've never read Ardis's blog, *Keepapitchinin*, this would be a good time to start. Not only is she a pro at ferreting out the most colorful characters in Mormon history, but she's uproariously funny as well. We guarantee it's a good read.

But back to topic—Ardis starts out her blog about the Mormon hooligans with this disclaimer: "I wish I could record it rather than posting the bare script—I get a kick out of teasing laughs from the audience by the style of delivery. What can I say? I'm a ham." Absent an audio button, we'll have to tell the story here much as she did, so try to "hear" it as she'd want you to.

First, a little background on the major characters in the scandalous skirmish: Andrew Balfour Hepburn and James Marsden, not exactly household names. Oh, wait—there is a dashingly handsome actor and former Versace model prancing around this very minute named James Marsden. You may have seen him on TV as well as on the silver screen. His actually *is* a household name. But he's not the one who figured so prominently in our outrageous skirmish . . . that one definitely *isn't* a household name.

But we digress.

Our James Marsden was born in Derbyshire, England, in 1827. He joined the Church when he was fourteen, and at the tender age of nineteen, he was already the branch president in Liverpool. This was a boy who let no moss grow under his feet.

By the time James Marsden was twenty-three—in 1850—he was called to be the president of the Edinburgh Conference. That's roughly the equivalent of a stake president. At twenty-three. In 1854, when our story takes place, he was twenty-seven and already responsible for providing spiritual care to roughly four thousand members of the Church in the London area. You'd think this was a young man who had a bright and involved future in the Church.

That year James was sharing a London apartment with a pair of middle-aged missionaries—William Henry Kimball, son of Apostle Heber C. Kimball, and William Warner Major, a painter of some renown. (Nine years earlier Heber C. Kimball had hired Major to paint a portrait of his family, which included William Henry Kimball, his wife, and their young daughter.[2])

The three became fast friends, as roommates often do. Then Major fell ill. His long-time friend and missionary companion, William Henry Kimball, stayed at his side during his protracted illness, and was completely anguished when Major died at 7 p.m. on October 2, 1854. After all, the two had been close friends since Kimball was nineteen. At the death, Kimball wrote his father, "Through this bereavement I feel as lonely as though there was not a person within a thousand miles of me."[3]

James Marsden wasn't nearly as close to William Major as Kimball was—after all, they had met for the first time when becoming roommates in 1853. Nevertheless, Marsden took chief responsibility for writing a not-very-epic history of William Warner Major, a tome he completed just after the painter's death.

Apparently James was a cracker-jack Church leader, but he doesn't seem to have been necessarily devoted to the facts.

On October 11, 1854—just nine days after Major's death—William H. Kimball wrote in his missionary journal, "Went to Elder Marston's and got the history of Elder Major as near as possible and sent it to Liverpool."[4] Go ahead and read between the lines of that brief journal entry. Obviously, Kimball had moved out of the apartment he had previously shared with James. And, just as obviously, his descriptor of the history—*as near as possible*—indicates that he had some doubts as to the accuracy of that history.

Sure enough, James Marsden had taken some liberties with the facts. And, unfortunately, those "imprecise statements," according to Jill C. Major, endured for more than 145 years—until she took the time to correct and explain.

Some of the "imprecise statements" aren't necessarily too earth-shaking. For instance, James wrote that Major had been ordained an elder soon after his baptism and was sent on a mission to Reading, where he "was successful in bringing many persons into the Church." Actually, he spent most of his mission in Newbury, not Reading, and the "many persons" translated to thirty-three.[5]

Some were a bit more serious. James writes that Major immigrated to Nauvoo and arrived in there "about the month of August" in 1844. Actually, William Warner Major landed in Nauvoo on April 18, 1844, aboard the steamer *Hugh Patrick*, which had left New Orleans on April 5. Oh, well . . . what's four months, give or take?[6] A number of other dates were also misreported.

And while we won't go into detail, some of the other "facts" in the history were a bit more seriously contorted. You do have to give James snaps, however, for the eloquent way in which he concluded the pithy history: "Such is a brief outline of the career of this faithful messenger of truth. It seems hard that he should die so far from home and friends, but this will serve to enhance his fame and brighten his crown. He fell while fighting the battle of truth. He fell honourably, nobly. He fell to rise again, for his title is divine, and he maintained it inviolate to the last."

That should do for a background on James Marsden. Now for the hooligan in our story: Andrew Balfour Hepburn, who was thirty-nine years old at the time. While we don't have his birth date, Andrew was christened on December 28, 1815, in Linlithgow, West Lothian, Scotland; his parents were John Hepburn, a soldier, and Christian Doughty. (Christian was the mother.)

Ardis Parshall fills in some of the more juicy details about Andrew for us:

Most of what is known about his background comes from his own account, not from unflattering stories by irritated British Mormons. He tells us that as a child he "positively refused to go to school," and that after he had been apprenticed to a weaver, he was so unruly that his master "took [him] before the justices no less than four different times, for disobedience." Failing to receive the services he had contracted for, the weaver discharged Hepburn before his time. The young man then found employment as a farm laborer, but he rebelled against the farmer who "called me up at five o'clock in the morning." For this unconscionable action of the farmer, and, "not exactly liking this out-door labour which I considered rather menial," Hepburn left the farmer.[7]

After that, Andrew apparently worked from time to time as a weaver. He was also paid to be an informant for the Glasgow police department.

Andrew had been a member of the Church of Scotland until its factions separated, forming the Free Church. He determined that neither of them coincided with his views, even though he found "no fault with the gospel, as preached by either. I gave up attending both churches . . . making my own abode a 'house of prayer,' having family worship regularly night and morning."[8]

In 1844—a decade before the episode of hooliganism in the British chapel—Andrew was baptized a member of the Church. While he entered the waters of baptism "with a good conscience,"[9] he wrote, he was by all intents and purposes ill-prepared for his baptism. He claims he didn't even hear about Joseph Smith or the Book of Mormon until eight days after he'd been baptized—and then he said it was from a family member. When he confronted the missionaries who had baptized him, they mumbled something about "milk" and "meat"—the Book of Mormon and Joseph Smith were the "meat" of the gospel, they said, and they had chosen to give him only what he was prepared to accept ("the milk").

At that, Andrew responded, "Then you have given me stronger meat than my weak stomach will be able to digest."

At that, the missionary squared up his shoulders and warned, "If you do not believe the gospel taught by the Book of Mormon, you will be damned."

Andrew had a dilemma on his hands: he says he didn't even *know* the gospel taught by the Book of Mormon. Heck, he didn't even know the Book of Mormon. And so, after an eight-day career in The Church of Jesus Christ of Latter-day Saints, he left said church.

You know how much trouble he'd had holding down a job? Well, Andrew's new "job" was to bad-mouth the Church. And he was good at it. To start things off, he published two anti-Mormon pamphlets: *An exposition of the blasphemous doctrines and delusions of the so-called Latter-day Saints, or Mormons containing an authentic account of the impositions, spiritual wife doctrine, and the other abominable practices of Joseph Smith, the American Mahomet* (how's *that* for a title that will literally take your breath away?), and a two-part diatribe titled *Mormonism exploded, or, The religion of the Latter-day Saints proved to be a system of imposture, blasphemy and immorality with the autobiography and portrait of the author* (another succinct label).

But that's not all. At least as early as 1845, he staged "performances" (his word, not ours) in which he "exposed" the so-called foibles of Mormonism. He attracted full houses that often included newspaper reporters. By the time he reached London in February 1853, he had lectured (or "performed," as the case might be) in thirty-eight cities. For the next seventeen months, he conducted twice-a-week "lectures" in and around London.

And that's where we pick up our story. You see, Andrew didn't limit his lectures to the curious who were anxious to hear about the Mormons. As in the story we're about to tell, he often infiltrated Mormon meetings—like the one where the Saints of the Bethnal Green District of East London were meeting at No. 41 Globe Road.

Before we detail what happened at Globe Road, let's look at how missionaries of the day were often treated.[10] To put it mildly, nineteenth-century missionaries weren't exactly greeted with open arms when they arrived in town—any town. In the United States, the cradle of Mormonism, they were occasionally whipped and shot. In the Scandinavian countries, they were banished. In the German states, they were tossed in jail and *then* banished. Great Britain was a bit more civilized: there they were merely pelted with eggs, mud, and rotten tomatoes.

And it wasn't just the missionaries. As Ardis Parshall clarifies:

> [H]alls rented as Mormon meeting places sometimes had their windows broken. But Great Britain's special claim to missionary harassment took the form of hooliganism. Sure, rowdies in America did often throw stones at buildings where elders were preaching, and even shot through the walls on occasion—but the English raised hooliganism to a fine art, unrivaled elsewhere.[11]

The pattern of most of these "disturbances" was, in fact, disturbingly similar from one place to another. At the conclusion of a talk, the missionary would invite questions. And, oh, did the questions come—not politely, one or two at a time, but simultaneously, everyone shouting at once, until the missionary was completely dumbfounded. It was very much like a riot, as a matter of fact. Before it was all over, the audience would often throw all kinds of debris—even stuff as heavy as books and rocks—at the missionary until he just had to retreat to save life and limb. Needless to say, the meetings were never closed with prayer.

At one point, the missionaries tried to prevent such behavior by limiting attendance to the Saints and those who had been *invited* by the Saints. A bouncer of sorts stood at the door, questioning people about their credentials. Well, you can imagine how well *that* went over. People got so upset they started railing on the bouncer, and he was compelled to seek refuge inside the building. Even though the police were sent for, the usual riotous behavior ensued. While the missionary "manfully kept his ground," half the crowd sided with the Mormons and the other half clearly did not. As is written in Parshall's account, "A general fight ensued, bonnets were broken, coats torn, and hats smashed."

One such meeting ended particularly badly. When the mob outside heard all the commotion, a crowd of newcomers pressed into the hall. The ringleader who was hurling questions at the speaker got his coat slit up the back—by a Mormon. The knife-wielding Mormon, in return, was beat up. (Shouter, 1; Mormon, 0.) The police finally managed to restore order, but as they were leaving, the Mormons were bombarded with mud and rocks.

Makes today's meetings look absolutely benign. Unless you're having more scuffles in the parking lot than we are.

In all of these incidents, the police seem if not sympathetic to the Mormons' plight, at least determined to maintain order. They always responded quickly when called. In some cases, they stationed police at Mormon chapels and meeting places even *before* they were called, anticipating trouble—which always seemed to come. None of the episodes received any widespread attention among British society.

Until, that is, 1854.

You guessed it: enter Andrew Balfour Hepburn and James Marsden, head to head.

Here's how it started: On a balmy Sunday evening in August 1854, a London newspaper reporter was casually strolling through the town square when he came upon

> a man mounted upon a table haranguing pass-
> ers-by. The orator had a very large mouth, a
> Scotch accent, and a jocular stare. . . . I cannot

say that [his attire] was very shabby, but it was
clear that [he was ignorant] of the art of mend-
ing rags. . . . Nor was I quite certain that [he
was] in the habit of visiting baths, wash-houses,
or barbers' shops. . . . [He informed] the gaping
crowd that he had a special mission from heav-
en to expose the horrid errors of the followers
of Mormon the Prophet Joseph Smith. . . . I
could not help remarking that he was one of
the cleverest mob orators I had ever heard . . .
but, at the same time, it was clear he did not
understand his call from heaven to mean that
he should learn to speak the English language
with propriety or put aside rude and coarse
manners. . . . [T]he art which he had managed
to greatest perfection was that of plunging his
assembly into roars of laughter.

The shabbily dressed and barely groomed man spewing his
rhetoric from atop the table, of course, was our man, Andrew
Balfour Hepburn. He jumped down from the table and invited
the mobs who had gathered around to follow him to a meeting of
the Stepney LDS Branch.

Oh, boy. Fasten your seatbelt.

The Stepney Branch was meeting in a hall that had been
rented by one of the local Church members, thirty-seven-year-
old branch president James Harrison. President Harrison, an
engraver by trade, had been baptized three years earlier and
was a dependable chap who often conducted services when the
missionaries couldn't be there. Since he had been the one to lease
the hall, he was responsible for paying the rent—two guineas per
quarter. And here's the unfortunate part: he was also responsible
for any damage that was caused to the building or its furnishings.

We're sure you can see what's coming here.

Conducting the evening's meeting was our other man,
James Marsden, the twenty-seven-year-old conference president

(remember, that's roughly the equivalent of a stake president). Brief background: This wouldn't be the first time Marsden and Hepburn had encountered each other. During a meeting of the Poplar Branch in East London, Elder Marsden had been speaking when Hepburn leaped to his feet and demanded that Marsden stop. Marsden *didn't* stop—instead, he called on members of the congregation to throw Hepburn out of the hall. They did. Hepburn was furious.

He was so furious, in fact, that at a later meeting at Barking, Essex, Hepburn had been part of a mob outside the hall that had been trying to break the sound barrier with their noise and to intimidate the Saints inside. Suddenly, Hepburn thought he saw Marsden standing by the window. Animal instinct took over: Hepburn balled up his fist and punched it through the glass. The police were called. Hepburn was arrested. Hepburn was released on bail, but bolted. He was later captured by the police and fined for assault on Elder Marsden.

So, as is obvious, Elder James Marsden was less than thrilled on August 18, 1854, to see none other than Andrew Balfour Hepburn, who had managed to squeeze into the room with eighty or so other shouting mobsters. At the time, Marsden was quoting a passage from the Doctrine and Covenants. Brutish and loud, Hepburn began to heckle Marsden. The jeers got increasingly worse.

At this point, Marsden knew *exactly* what he was up against, and he asked a deacon in the branch to run to the police station around the corner. A policeman arrived immediately. After "considerable resistance" from Hepburn, the policeman was able to remove him from the hall.

That was just what Hepburn's throng needed to incite them to riot. With the policeman outside strong-arming Hepburn, the herd of rabble-rousers threw bricks through the skylight and broke the bell. (Poor James Harrison, who was on the line for all the damages.) One mobster stormed to the stand and attempted to take over the meeting. The Saints, knowing the meeting had come to an inglorious end, started filing out of the building. Hepburn, still restrained by the policeman, shouted that they hadn't seen the last of him—he would be at their meeting the following Friday night.

James Harrison—you know, the one who had to pay for the shattered skylight and broken bell—notified the police of Hepburn's threat. The police promised to be on the alert.

Sure enough, Hepburn made good on his threat. The mob repeated its assault on the meeting hall (who knows what else they broke) and harassed Marsden with new levels of malice. It took three policemen to subdue the horde. Hepburn was arrested and hauled to police court. A hearing was scheduled for three weeks later. Long story short, Hepburn was convicted of riot and assault and was sentenced to three months in jail.

Incidentally, the judge at the hearing was a real stand-up guy. When Hepburn started railing against the Church, the judge shut him down by reminding him that he was in a courtroom, not a chapel. Right on.

Similar events had happened many times before, and only once had there been much news commentary. This time was different. As Parshall described it, there was "a tsunami of press coverage." She wrote:

> I have found coverage so far in 41 newspapers in Great Britain, much of it multi-column editorials. Coverage started with the *Times* of London on the day after Hepburn's conviction, with a hand-wringing editorial opining that of course the English were a tolerant people, and of course the Mormons should be tolerated. But that did not mean they were eligible for the protections of the Protestant Dissenters law. "Tolerate, but do not protect," was its conclusion.

Other newspapers responded. "Religious freedom is a civil right," the Manchester *Times* retorted, "and what the *Times* means, if it means anything, is that this civil right should be denied to the Mormons."

Another London editor said: "We know how our liberty-loving friends on the other side of the Atlantic would have treated the question. They would have pulled down the meeting-house, shot the preacher, and . . . maltreated . . . the worshippers. . . . Here, however, we think it better to let folly run its course."

Despite the blistering editorial in the *Times*, the overwhelming position of the press came out on the other side. They may have deplored the presence of Mormonism in Britain, but they acknowledged that the Mormons had followed the law. If nothing else, the Brits were committed to fair play—and so, the press concluded, the Mormons were entitled to protection in their worship.

The commotion eventually died down. Hepburn served his three-month term. And life in the Stepney Branch pretty much returned to normal—maybe even a little better than normal, we hope.

And what of our two main players?

This likely won't surprise you. Fresh from his prison term, Andrew Hepburn resumed harassing the Mormons and disrupting their meetings. He was, as you would call it today, a repeat offender. He was arrested again in 1855, 1857, 1858, and 1859. One thing you have to say for him: he was consistent. Throughout his hooliganism, he repeatedly boasted of his term in prison as proof that he was having a "great effect" in society.

Andrew Balfour Hepburn died in London in July 1884.

And what about James Marsden?

That one's not nearly so neat and clean.

In 1854—the year of the now-famous uprising in the Stepney Branch—James Marsden was released from his eleven years of missionary and leadership service in the Church. He was expected to immediately emigrate to Zion. He didn't—probably, theorizes Parshall, because his wife didn't want to go to Utah.

Since he was still hanging around in England the next year, he was called in 1855 to head up the Liverpool Conference. Another stake president position. But we hope he didn't get too settled and comfy, because in late 1856 Brigham Young notified Orson Pratt, the mission president in Liverpool, that James Marsden's "labors are not needed in Europe, let him . . . come immediately to Zion, or be cut off from the Church."

Harsh. But straightforward.

When the Mormon emigration season kicked off in March 1857, James Marsden wasn't in line to climb aboard the ship bound for Zion. Accordingly, Apostle Ezra T. Benson wrote to Brigham Young:

> By your request we released . . . Mr James Marsden from his labours [in February] giving him instructions to prepare to go home. . . . [W]hen the day came for [the Mormon emigrant ship] to sail he . . . sent us a letter telling us he had declined emigrating. . . . —And for this . . . we excommunicated him from the church this day.[12]

Dang.

Despite his promising early start, James Marsden died outside the Church.

A group of LDS World War II servicement gather outside the chapel built by cigarettes on the Italian island of Sardinia.

MARVEL FARRELL ANDERSEN
THE CHAPEL BUILT BY CIGARETTES

YOU'VE PROBABLY NEVER HEARD OF Marvel Farrell Andersen.

That's understandable. There's not really any pressing reason why you would have.

Unless, of course, you happened to be on the Italian island of Sardinia during World War II . . . because that's where Marvel Farrell Andersen and a handful of his fellow Mormon soldiers managed to build a chapel of cigarettes.

Okay. Banish any images you have of a small group of hard-working Mormon infantrymen stacking up a zillion cigarettes and gluing them together to form walls and a roof—and, don't forget, the steeple. (*Good until the first time it rains,* you might be thinking.) Because that's not exactly what we mean. But what really *did* happen is pretty darn cool.

Marvel Farrell Andersen was born January 2, 1908, in Vineyard, Utah[1]—at the time not much more than a sleepy little farming community west of Orem. His parents, James X. and Petrea Thyrring Andersen, had both immigrated to the United States from Denmark. About the time the stock market crashed, kicking off the Great Depression, Marvel was on his way to England, where he served an LDS mission from 1929 through 1930.

We next see Marvel while the Allies and the Axis were duking it out in World War II: he served in the US Army Air Force as a sergeant in the 439th Bomber Squadron. And, as it turns out, he was right in the middle of the action.[2] In more ways than one.

In the summer of 1943, the American and British armies landed on the island of Sicily in southern Italy and started the arduous task of ramming the German army northward, eventually bullying them right out of the country. Air support was critical to a successful campaign, so the US Air Force established two hulking airfields on the Italian island of Sardinia. From those airfields, the air force could launch its state-of-the-art B-26 "Marauder" bombers.

Marvel Farrell Andersen was stationed on Sardinia and found himself there with a few dozen other LDS servicemen who, despite the rigors of their military commitments, wanted to meet as often as they could on Sundays. Writing home on February 12, 1944, Marvel said that although they didn't have many out for their first meeting, they seemed to "get along fine." Marvel told his folks that he had presided on the previous Sunday; following the sacrament, the three of them who were there had all given talks and sung songs.

Three? Yeah, that's not "many." But it was a start. And, hey, they also had a visitor: LDS Chaplain Eldin Ricks (originally from Idaho and later a professor of religion at Brigham Young University) had dropped by to worship with the airmen. Ricks, who had been required as a chaplain to specify whether he was Catholic or Protestant, worried about how to find the LDS kids who were serving. Instead, he made it easy for *them* to find *him*: he painted a beehive and the word *Deseret* on the sides of his jeep.[3] His artwork meant nothing to the vast majority of military men and women but helped the LDS ones immediately find him.

Marvel told his parents that he had not only presided over the meeting but had given the blessing on the water and had offered the closing prayer. And his talk, he exulted, lasted for twenty minutes. In concluding his letter home, he wrote, "We will probably have more members out from now on. At least I hope so. We are studying the book *Jesus the Christ*. It seems good to get together and have a good meeting."

The very next day, the three LDS servicemen put their heads together and decided they needed a place where they could meet for regular church meetings. Writing home again on February 14, Marvel told his family they had all decided to "put in a few dollars and build a brick chapel in which to meet." Their numbers had swelled to six, and Marvel figured it wouldn't be too hard for the six of them to build what would be the first LDS meetinghouse in Sardinia—and as it would turn out, though they didn't know it at the time, the first in all of Italy.

Marvel was filled with excitement as he imagined the building, telling his parents that "we were thinking of getting a few fair-sized pictures of the First Presidency, and of Joseph and Hyrum Smith, and a couple of *Deseret Song Books* so we can use them. So if you have any chance to see any of them, and it isn't too much trouble, I would like you to send them to me. There is a good need for them to decorate our place up with."

For Marvel, seeing was believing: he pictured that chapel so vividly in his mind that it might as well have been standing in front of him. He even arranged with a Captain Owen Ken Earl from Nevada to donate his portable organ—something, he wrote his parents, they would be able to use "to a very good advantage."

And once they had a permanent meetinghouse, Marvel figured, their numbers would enlarge even more. "We will probably have 25 to 50 fellows who we can get to come out and join us, and perhaps do a lot of good," he wrote in that same February 14 letter.

And so the boys set out to determine what building materials they could procure on the island. Let's just say there was good news, and there was bad news. The good news? Other than lumber, building supplies and labor were readily available on Sardinia, even during wartime. The bad news? They were available at a price—and the price was high. Much higher than our six gallant servicemen were able to scrape together.

And then a brilliant idea occurred to Marvel and his friends: what about their cigarettes?

All American servicemen got weekly rations that included a generous supply of cigarettes. The LDS men and women didn't smoke, of course, so they'd been simply giving their rations away to those who *did*.

What if they could barter their weekly rations of cigarettes for the supplies and labor they needed to construct their chapel? After poking around a bit and talking to island suppliers and laborers, they learned that the cigarettes made of American tobacco might as well have been gold. People were *delighted* to get the cigarettes in exchange for just about anything. With that, construction immediately started in earnest.

Writing to his parents on February 28, 1944—two weeks after first hatching the ingenious plan—Marvel said:

> Last night we had another good meeting and had a couple more out—that made eight of us. It seems as if each week we get another one or two. We are starting to build our chapel this week. We may have it done by next Sunday. I surely hope so. Then we can get a few more out, and we will have a nicer time. I'll take a few pictures of it, and send them to you when the chapel is completed.

Marvel's estimation of a week for the construction of the chapel was, not surprisingly, a bit optimistic. On March 10, almost two weeks later, he wrote that while the chapel was "almost finished," they wouldn't be able to move into it for another week. He exulted about how nice-looking it was and said he was going in to town the next day to try to find glass windows that could be set in the frames.

But probably his most exciting news was yet another boost in their numbers: with the promise of a nice place in which to meet, interest was piquing among the other LDS servicemen. "At last week's meeting we had twelve fellows out," he wrote. "That wasn't so bad, was it? We keep getting more each week."

The builders faced just one more obstacle: they needed lumber for the center beam and rafters—and lumber simply wasn't available on the island. No worry. The soldiers showed up on site with a perfect piece of lumber: a telephone pole. The builders sawed the hefty pole down the center, creating a center beam with one half and rafters with the other.

By March 27, the chapel was finished. There's no denying that it was tiny: measuring only twelve by twenty feet, it was just large enough to seat about twenty-five men in rows of four with a narrow center aisle and a tiny podium. But the soldiers were thrilled: it was all they needed and all of which they had ever dreamed. The attractive stucco building had a roof of red Mediterranean tile and a requisite steeple.

Marvel wrote home that night, saying they had "opened our new chapel and had quite a nice time. We had the organ and that helped quite a lot." He said that they hoped to get the chaplain over from Italy the next week.

Upon receiving their invitation, Chaplain Ricks addressed a circular to all the LDS servicemen under him:

> Good news came unexpectedly from Sardinia a few days ago in the form of an invitation to dedicate a chapel that the small group of L.D.S. men on the island have just finished building. It is an attractive little stucco type structure with a tile roof, cement floor, a seating capacity of about twenty-five, a gasoline stove, and electric lights. . . . They finished it by contributing from the group and by pooling their cigarette rations which, they explained, seemed to have a most remarkable buying power. They are to be congratulated for their resourcefulness and faith and also for building what probably is the first permanent L.D.S. chapel in Italy.

Chaplain Eldin Ricks dedicated the chapel on April 2, 1944.

Here's a bit of a melancholy note: the little LDS chapel built by cigarettes was used for only about five months. In September 1944, the American forces were moved from the Decimomannu airfield, where the chapel had been constructed, to those that were nearer the action to the north. The Decimomannu airfield is now a NATO base, and a broad, paved road now covers the site where the first chapel to be dedicated in Italy once stood.

And what of Marvel? He married Ruth Woodward on June 23, 1944, and the couple went on to have three children and seven grandchildren. He retired as a field representative for Federal National Mortgage Association in 1969, after which he worked for Western Mortgage and Loan until 1977. He died February 24, 1991.

Oh, and don't forget—once upon a time, in a faraway place, he built a chapel with cigarettes.

Mary Ann Angell Young, whose faith and determination drove her to strike out on her own and walk 251 miles to meet a prophet, never knowing ahead of time she'd also meet her man.

MARY ANN ANGELL YOUNG
DOING THE SPINSTER SHUFFLE

THE POINT AT WHICH MOST really come to know anything about Mary Ann Angell is when she, at the then-wizened age of thirty-one, married Brigham Young—the man who would become a prophet, governor, colonizer, and "lion of the Lord." But he was none of that stuff when Mary Ann Angell took a chance on him. And Mary Ann herself might have been considered a bit risky, being what society at the time ingloriously called a *spinster*.

So maybe you could say that Brigham Young took a chance on *her*.

Here's the deal: back in the day, any women who was still single past the usual marriageable age (and, dang, it was *young* back then) was classified as a *spinster*. The word was also used to describe a woman who had never been married—or, worst of all, a woman who seemed unlikely to marry. (Don't know quite who judged that.)

In fact, in Mary Ann Angell's day, "the spinster was either pitiable or contemptible, simply because of her spinsterhood. . . . [Marriage] was the great object of every woman, and she who did not attain to it was a complete failure."[1]

But here's the awesome thing about Mary Ann: she refused to cave to the pressure of having to get married or, as an alternative, being put out to pasture. A deeply religious woman who fervently studied both Hebrew and Christian scriptures, she vowed to never marry until she met "a man of God"—someone in whom she could confide her religious leanings and with whom she could actively unite in living a Christian life.[2]

So no bullyragging Mary Ann Angell just because she was . . . well, older and still not married. She knew what she was looking for, and, quite frankly, she'd rather be put out to pasture (and even called that derogatory term *spinster*) than be married to an inferior man who didn't meet her stringent standards.

Even though most of us don't know much about her until her marriage to Brigham Young, that's obviously not where her life started—and to pick it up there is to miss some of the uniquely colorful aspects that made her a woman of such fortitude.

So let's start at the beginning. Mary Ann Angell was born June 8, 1803, at Seneca, New York, to God-fearing parents James and Phoebe Morton Angell. When she was quite young, James and Phoebe moved their family to Providence, Rhode Island, where Mary Ann spent her childhood and young adulthood.

It was in Providence that Mary Ann joined the Free Will Baptist Church—a church dedicated to the theologies of free grace, free salvation, and free will. Church leaders taught that people are saved by faith and kept by faith. They also taught that the Bible, a book completely without error, was the very word of God; that there was a general Atonement; and that it was possible to willfully reject one's faith—in other words, to commit apostasy.

Like her parents, Mary Ann swiftly accepted the doctrines of her new church and became a Sunday school teacher. She continued to study the scriptures voraciously, acquiring a keen interest in the Bible. In fact, her study of the scriptures "so engrossed her mind, that she confidently looked for their fulfillment, in consequence of which she resolved never to marry until she should 'meet a man of God.'"[3]

It was also in Providence that Mary Ann's life suddenly took a turn and got very interesting indeed. In 1830, Elder Thomas B. Marsh came upon the scene, preaching about the Restoration of the true gospel. The preaching itself was undoubtedly of interest to Mary Ann, but remember: this was a girl who relished the scriptures. Elder Marsh preached from a bound book he called the Book of Mormon—and, much to her delight, it was a book of *scripture*. She immediately asked him for a copy of the book, and when it arrived, she devoured it. Every word.

Mary Ann accepted the famous challenge to pray about the truthfulness of the book, and she quickly developed a testimony of it as the word of God. In actuality, she didn't even need to read it to know it was true. Her biographer, Emmeline B. Wells, wrote, "She testified many times that the Spirit bore witness to her when she took the Book of Mormon in her hands, of the truth of its origin, so strongly that she could never afterwards doubt it."[4]

At about that time, Mary Ann's parents moved to the city of China, New York, and soon afterward, they traveled to Palmyra to visit friends. Well, you can just imagine what happened in Palmyra. Her parents were learning all about the Church but were not passing enough details along in their letters to satisfy Mary Ann. So she and her brother, Truman—who would later become the architect of the Salt Lake Temple—joined their parents in Palmyra to see for themselves what all the excitement was about.

They all embraced the gospel. And in 1832, they were all baptized by Elder John P. Greene, the brother-in-law of Brigham Young. And as you know, Brigham Young later figured prominently in Mary Ann's story.

Following her baptism, Mary Ann wanted to join the main body of the Saints in Kirtland, Ohio, but her parents weren't ready to go. No matter for Mary Ann. She may have been a spinster, but she was plucky—and determined. She set out for Kirtland on her own. This wasn't a mere jaunt down the lane; it was 251 miles, a considerable undertaking for *anyone*, let alone a single woman. But Mary Ann Angell never let a little thing like 251 miles get in her way. When she arrived in Kirtland at the age of thirty-one, she met Brigham Young. Sparks flew. There he was, Mary Ann's "man of God." And we guess you could say that the rest was history.

As soon as she heard Brigham Young preach, Mary Ann "instinctively felt drawn towards him, and . . . admired him so much, that when . . . he asked her to be his wife she unhesitatingly consented, feeling confident he was her true mate."[5]

After a whirlwind courtship, Brigham married Mary Ann Angell on February 18, 1834. A year and a half earlier, Brigham's first wife, Miriam Works, had died of chronic tuberculosis on September 8, 1832, leaving him with two young daughters. Brigham Young was clearly grateful for his new wife, writing in his diary that she "took charge of my children, kept my house, and labored faithfully for the interest of my family and the kingdom."[6]

Mary Ann was no longer a spinster and had found the man of God for whom she had waited so long. Brigham once again had a wife who was a mother to his children. It was truly a match made in heaven.

As happy as she was, things weren't exactly easy for Mary Ann. In the first place, she had scarcely had time to organize the house when Brigham left, marching with Zion's Camp from Kirtland to Clay County, Missouri. While the march—intended to regain land and possessions taken from the Mormons—was acknowledged as a training ground for future Church leaders, it was blisteringly difficult. And Mary Ann wasn't stupid; she realized her husband's life was at risk during much of the journey.

Problems and persecutions continued to rage, and Brigham often seemed to be at the heart of it all. In December 1837 Joseph Smith pruned about fifty loud and violent dissenters from the Church; all were men that Brigham had publicly testified against in defense of the Prophet. With that, Brigham's life was in peril, and he fled Kirtland on December 22. Joseph Smith and a host of faithful Church members were close on his heels.

But not Mary Ann. She stayed behind in Kirtland with the children. It turned out to be a very unpleasant winter. Apostates regularly terrorized her, ransacking her house with claims that Mary Ann was hiding Brigham. These ruffians were some of the worst of the worst, it appears. The tormentors "used 'threats and vile language' that undid [Mary Ann's] emotions until her health became frail. This was, she later told her biographer, 'undoubtedly the severest trial of my life.'"[7] And she had lots of pretty rough trials.

By February, Mary Ann could stand it no longer. Suffering from "consumption"—tuberculosis, the same ailment that had claimed Brigham's first wife—she gathered up the few things the mob hadn't taken and put everything else behind her, traveling with her children to join Brigham in Richmond, Missouri. It was the second time the indomitable Mary Ann had struck out on her own; this time, she clocked 792 miles. Just imagine a lone woman—and a sick one at that—going that distance while trying to care for a handful of little children.

It was, needless to say, a long and difficult journey. In fact, when she finally arrived at her destination, Brigham was so shocked at the change in Mary Ann's appearance that he cried, "You look as if you were almost in your grave."[8] Having already lost one wife to tuberculosis, it's not hard to imagine how distressed Brigham Young was to see his second one similarly afflicted.

Brigham knew that he needed to focus on nursing his wife back to health, and it seems the Lord saw it that way too. On April 17, 1838, Joseph Smith received a revelation temporarily relieving Brigham from his substantial Church responsibilities.[9] It was time for him to focus on Mary Ann.

But Mary Ann scarcely had time to lie around on the sofa eating bonbons. Within a very short time, mob hostilities whipped back up, and by October Church members were expelled from their homes. Brigham and Mary Ann were among the number who left Far West in the bitter cold to seek refuge in Quincy, Illinois; most had to walk, since mobs had taken their animals and wagons.

But let's be clear about what happened: Brigham and Mary Ann didn't leave Far West *together*. Oh, no; Brigham had to go ahead so he could help the poor and needy get out of Missouri. Lives were at stake. Perhaps Brigham didn't even question that his wife would have the nerve and wherewithal to make it out without his help.

Mary Ann's descendant Laura P. Angell King tells what happened next. Sensing it was now or never, Mary Ann secured a wagon, put a few necessities in it, and hired an elder to help her get away. By now, there were five children in the family who were under her care; Brigham Young Jr. and his twin sister, Mary, were just babies. Mary Ann climbed into the wagon, seated herself on top of the load, and cradled a baby in each arm.

They had no longer started out than the wagon hit a deep rut in the road. It was every parent's worst nightmare: Mary Ann's baby girl was thrown out of her arm and slammed onto the road, where the wagon wheel passed over her head. The driver hopped off his horse, picked up the little girl, and said, "This poor little thing will surely die." For all intents and purposes, it seemed he was right—Mary's head was crushed.

And what of Mary Ann? She didn't scream. She didn't faint. Instead, she snatched her baby girl out of the driver's hands and commanded him, "Don't prophesy evil, brother; take the other child." With skillful hands, she pressed the little head back into shape, all the while praying desperately that God would spare her baby.

At last she climbed back onto the wagon, cradling her babies in her arms, and signaled the driver to go forward. Two days later they met Brigham Young; by then, his baby girl was fine.

Brigham found temporary housing for his family—a stable that he whitewashed and cleaned up. His family shared the stable with Orson Pratt and his family. Once Brigham had Mary Ann and the children settled in temporary lodging, he went back to help the poorest of the Saints press onward. But the whitewashed stable was hardly the only place Mary Ann inhabited. In just a three-month period, Mary Ann and the children lived in *eleven* different quarters. Good thing she was determined.

Fewer than six months later, Mary Ann gave birth to Emma Alice on September 4, 1839, in Montrose, Iowa Territory. Ten days later, Brigham had to leave again, this time on a mission to England. Brigham was so ill that he couldn't walk unassisted to the river to board the boat that would take him on the first leg of his journey to England. He wasn't alone; Mary Ann and the children were all sick too. It wasn't the greatest time to be launching out on another great adventure.

Summoning up all her strength, Mary Ann managed to get across the river. She wanted the chance to hold Brigham in her arms one more time before he left for a foreign country. Want to know the kind of grit she always displayed? Taking him in her arms, Mary Ann told him, "Go and fill your mission, and the Lord will bless you, and I will do the best I can for myself and the children."[10]

That's exactly what she did—though the going was often tougher than she or anyone else could have anticipated.

How about this for an example of what Mary Ann often faced: between her home in Montrose and the city of Nauvoo, the Mississippi River was a mile wide. Yet she often had to make the dangerous trek across the river on a flimsy skiff in order to get food.

One day late in November 1839, Mary Ann was desperately sick with malaria. (You'll recall that Nauvoo was nothing more than a mosquito-infested swamp when the Saints first settled there.) All of her children were so hungry they were crying for food.

On a good day in November, the weather at the Mississippi crossing is cold. Really cold. When a storm whips up, it can be downright brutal. A winter storm had descended, sweeping a bitter northwesterly wind across the river. But Mary Ann had no choice: their survival depended on her ability to get food.

Wearing only a thin cotton dress and a shawl, Mary Ann wrapped a ragged blanket around herself and her baby, Emma Alice. She threw another tattered blanket into the boat and, summoning all the resolve she could, she rowed into wind-whipped waves that soaked both her and her baby to the skin.

Arriving in Nauvoo—undoubtedly a sight for sore eyes—Mary Ann staggered to the home of a friend, who took her in and fed her. Noting that Mary Ann was "almost fainting with cold and hunger, and dripping wet," the friend tried to persuade her to stay, as anyone would. "But she refused, saying, 'the children at home are hungry, too.' I shall never forget how she looked, shivering with cold and thinly clad. . . . She came back [from the tithing office] with a few potatoes and a little flour, for which she seemed very grateful, and . . . weak as she was from ague [malaria] and fever, wended her way to the river bank to row home again."[11]

As it turns out, Mary Ann had an unusual gift for healing—as evidenced by her rescue of her baby girl—and it was a gift she supplemented with dedicated study of herbal and folk remedies. Little did she know how colorful her life was about to get and how much her "medical" knowledge would bless her and the many others she would encounter.

And little did she know she would be the first to try a technique that would not be used—or even known about—until sometime during the twentieth century.

It happened like this: As Brigham was returning from his mission to England, he fell desperately sick with what seemed to be scarlet fever. Without antibiotics to kill the strep infection, it was extremely serious; patients were quarantined for long periods of time, and many died of the infection.

In his weakened and ailing condition, he arrived home in the middle of winter; Mary Ann and the children were living in a log cabin that had nothing more than a blanket for a door. Not exactly the ideal conditions in which to recover from severe illness. Nonetheless, Mary Ann put Brigham to bed and nursed him the best she could.

The fever finally broke on the eighteenth day—by then, Brigham wrote, "I was bolstered up in my chair, but was so near gone that I could not close my eyes, which were set in my head. My chin dropped down and my breath stopped. My wife, seeing my situation, threw cold water in my face, which I did not feel; neither did I move a muscle." Desperate times really do call for desperate measures, and trust Mary Ann to know what to do. Continuing his account, Brigham wrote that Mary Ann "dashed a handful of strong camphor into my face and eyes, which I did not feel in the least."[12]

When that didn't snap him out of it, according to Laura P. Angell King, Brigham wrote that Mary Ann "then held my nostrils between her thumb and finger, and placing her mouth directly over mine, blew into my lungs until she filled them with air. This set my lungs in motion, and I again began to breathe. While this was going on, I was perfectly conscious of all that was passing around me; my spirit was as vivid as it ever was, but I had no feeling in my body."

We know it, of course, as artificial respiration—a resuscitative technique commonly used today but not really "discovered" until the twentieth century—long after Mary Ann performed it on her husband.

Settled in Nauvoo, Mary Ann initially enjoyed a sense of peace and calm. But before long, the Prophet was martyred and the Saints were forced once again from their homes—yet again in the worst possible winter weather. In the interim, Mary Ann had made it a point to continue studying folk medicine and herbal remedies, and it was knowledge she would put to good use as the pioneers made their way west to Utah.

Brigham left Winter Quarters, Nebraska, with the vanguard company in 1847, but Mary Ann initially stayed behind to care for the children and a number of others who couldn't make the trek that first summer. Three weeks after arriving in the Salt Lake Valley—once he had the initial wave of exhausted pioneers settled—Brigham started back out across the plains to get Mary Ann and the rest of his family. Together, they arrived in Salt Lake on September 20, 1848.

While they were in Winter Quarters, there was sickness in almost every log cabin in the settlement, wrote Mary Ann's biographer—with virtually no comforts and completely scarce provisions. "Inquiring into their needs and bestowing medicine and attention whenever she could," Mary Ann was "an angel of mercy in very deed."[13]

It was during the trek that Mary Ann really put her knowledge to work. There were both highlights and lowlights. For example, Mary Ann had a few pioneer celebrities among her patients. At one point, she restored Eliza R. Snow to health. On another occasion, she nursed Colonel Thomas L. Kane back to health; he went on to help and defend the Saints through quite a few unpredictable situations. But it wasn't just the celebs that she tended; she used her talents and gift for healing on many a careworn pioneer along the trail.

In addition to the precious herbal remedies she carried along the trail, Mary Ann brought a variety of seeds with her to the Salt Lake Valley. It was she who planted the magnificent trees along the east end of South Temple Street in Salt Lake City—at first fittingly known as Brigham Street.

Mary Ann, once considered a spinster, ended up with a large and prominent family. She bore six children and cared for her two adopted daughters for the rest of her life. And her children read like a "who's who" of early Church history. Brigham Young Jr. was ordained an Apostle and served in the Quorum of the Twelve. Another son, John Willard Young, was ordained an Apostle and was first counselor to his father in the First Presidency. Still another son, Joseph Angell Young, was also ordained an Apostle, though he did not serve as a member of the Twelve or the First Presidency.

And her daughter Eunice Caroline Young married George Washington Thatcher; together, they managed a wealthy family organization and a number of Brigham Young's business enterprises in Cache Valley and Logan, Utah.

Mary Ann was no slouch, either. LDS church historian Andrew Jenson wrote of her, "She was a very gifted and intelligent woman, highly cultured, yet humble and meek, ever ready to help the poor and needy, or ease the suffering of the afflicted. She passed through great trials and privation, but through it all she was a faithful wife, model mother, and Latter-day Saint, in whose heart native goodness and benevolence abounded."

By the time Brigham Young died in 1877, Mary Ann's health had become fairly shaky. She suffered a number of physical ailments that, over the ensuing few years, began to cause her severe pain. But Mary Ann had never been one to whine or complain, even through all the disasters she endured, and she bore her physical infirmities the same way—with "great patience and the most perfect resignation to the will of her heavenly Father."[14] As her biographer wrote, she passed through the worst of all hardships with extraordinary acceptance, "always [looking] upward from whence help would come."[15]

Mary Ann Angell Young, the "spinster" who held out for what she wanted and found her "man of God" in a young father with two little girls, survived her husband by almost five years. She died on June 27, 1882, in Salt Lake City at the age of seventy-nine.

Orson Pratt Jr.—was he in or was he out?

Orson Pratt Jr.
Sometimes You Feel Like a Saint, Sometimes You Don't

Mormon Church history is brimming with examples of boys who grew up to follow their famous Church-leader fathers into the hierarchy of Church leadership; they include men like Brigham Young Jr., Joseph F. Smith, Heber J. Grant, John Henry Smith, John W. Taylor, Abraham O. Woodruff, and Abraham H. Cannon, to name a few.[1]

That list does *not* include Orson Pratt Jr.

Oh, he *seemed* to be going along in the same direction as the others until he made a shocking announcement in 1864. Just stick with us, and you'll find out why his announcement came as such an outrage.

Orson Pratt Jr. was born July 11, 1837, in Kirtland, Ohio, to Orson Pratt and Sarah M. Bates. He had the distinction not only of being his father's namesake, but of being the firstborn of Pratt's forty-five children. Orson Sr., who had been baptized at the age of nineteen, was the younger brother of Parley P. Pratt. It was quite a legacy as far as legacies go.

During the early days of the Church, no one seemed to stay put in any one place for very long, and the Pratt family was no exception. When the Kirtland Safety Society—a banking and joint stock company—bit the dust in 1837 on the heels of a national banking crisis, the Pratts moved to Henderson, New York, where they stayed only briefly before embarking on a series of equally brief moves to St. Louis, Missouri; Quincy, Illinois; and Montrose, Iowa. They finally settled in Nauvoo, Illinois, in 1839. That's a lot of moves in just fewer than two years, and it's easy to figure that Orson Jr. suffered some collateral damage as a result.

Just five years later the Prophet Joseph Smith was martyred, and things started going south in Nauvoo. Along with most of the rest of the Saints, Orson Pratt gathered up his family and started out on the trek west. At some point in the beginning of their journey, he and the family decided to temporarily part ways. Orson—by that time a member of the Quorum of the Twelve—left his family in Winter Quarters, Nebraska, for the time being while he continued on to Salt Lake with the vanguard pioneer company of 1847.

Orson wasn't in Salt Lake for long when he was called on April 16, 1848, as mission president to preside over all the branches of the Church in Europe. Along with that substantial responsibility, he was called to edit the *Millennial Star*, a Church periodical published initially in Manchester, England, in 1840 but which moved to Liverpool in 1842. Orson's brother Parley had been the original editor, but when the paper made its move to Liverpool, the mission presidents got the task of editing the periodical. Now it was Orson's turn. (Point of interest: the *Millennial Star* became the longest continually published periodical in the Church, being published from 1840 to 1970, when it was replaced by the Church-wide *Ensign*. You know the one.)

As he packed his bags for England, he made plans to swing by Winter Quarters and pick up his family, who was still hanging out in Nebraska. And so it was that Orson, Sarah, and their three children left Winter Quarters on July 11 and arrived in Liverpool on July 26.

The three years that the Pratts spent in England were exciting times for Orson Jr. As would be expected, he attended school; as might not necessarily be expected, he was given excellent musical training under some of the best musicians in Europe. It was training that would serve him well later in his life—but let's not get ahead of ourselves.

England also proved exciting to young Orson because he was allowed to help his father go door to door distributing missionary tracts—but his enthusiasm wasn't because of what you might think. Oh, no. As he later said, his thrill came "not because I knew anything of what I was doing, but because I liked to see the old women, when they slammed the door, or threw the tracts into the streets in their anger."[2] Oh, well; boys will be boys. And maybe, just maybe, that should have been a bit of a red flag if anyone had known about it.

The Pratts returned to the United States in early 1851. In Kanesville, Iowa, they got outfitted for the trip across the plains to Utah; for Orson Sr., it would be his second trek across the prairie, so this time he hired a team of thirteen strapping—but very inexperienced—young men to drive his company to Utah.

The raw, inexpert guides weren't the only problem. Unfortunately, the cattle were wild. Let's just say that many of the wagons tipped over and were damaged (along with plenty of their contents) during the three months it took them to slog across the prairie.

Orson Jr. especially remembered some cataclysmically wild adventures. On one occasion, the wagon train pulled perilously close to a herd of buffalo. The chance was just too good to pass up for one of the men, who thoughtlessly shot at a buffalo. The massive, startled animals reared at the sound of the gunshot and, snorting for all they were worth, stampeded between the wagons. Fortunately, no one was injured.

A short time later, while camped on the banks of the Sweetwater River in Wyoming, the company's own cattle—you remember, the wild ones—were stampeded by Indians. At that point, Sarah, who was eight months pregnant, had just about reached her limit when it came to adventure. And so it was that while the cattle were being rounded up, she decided to strike out on her own for a while, sort of a little time-out to gather her wits. She secured a carriage and set out with fourteen-year-old Orson Jr. and his nine-year-old sister, Celestia.

But things didn't quite go as Sarah had anticipated. As soon as the carriage was safely out of sight of the company—with the men still scrambling to round up those renegade cattle—an Indian, knife in hand, leaped from the brush, grabbed the horse's bit, and tried to cut the animal loose. All those stories you've heard about Indians stealing horses? This was one of them. And just imagine how Orson Jr. must have felt.

In this case, at least, Sarah was one lucky woman. She hadn't noticed before, but her brother, Ormus Bates, had seen her making a getaway and had decided to follow her. Seeing the Indian attack, Ormus bounded off his horse and started running toward the Indian. Realizing he now had more opposition than a hapless pregnant woman in a carriage with two young children, the Indian fled the scene.

At last the beleaguered group neared their destination. On October 6, 1851, Orson Jr. got his first glimpse of Salt Lake City from Big Mountain when his father cried, "All get out and have a view of the city!"[3] After what they'd been through, it had to be a sight for sore eyes. The next day they drove their wagons to Temple Square, where they camped out for two weeks before claiming their section of a property previously developed by Parley P. Pratt. The patch of dirt on which they built their home is where Salt Lake City's Marriott Hotel now stands.

Things were still going well for Orson Jr. as far as the Church was concerned—at least, it *seems* so. On March 1, 1852, fourteen-year-old Orson Jr. was endowed in the Endowment House,[4] the forerunner of the Salt Lake Temple. On July 22 of that same year, Orson Pratt Sr. did what all the other newly arrived Saints customarily did: he rebaptized his entire family,[5] an ordinance that signaled their continued dedication to the Church. (This practice, which started in Nauvoo and resumed in the Utah Territory, was discontinued in 1897.[6])

A month later, Orson Sr. was sent on a mission to the eastern United States to publish *The Seer*, a periodical that advocated polygamy. It could have been a bit of a dicey assignment for Orson, who—along with his wife, Sarah—originally opposed the concept of plural marriage. However, Orson later modified his position and eventually married nine additional wives. So he seemed to be good with his new assignment.

Maybe the assignment *was* a little too dicey for Sarah, though, because that's when things really started to go south in the Pratt household. A series of what Sarah considered to be scuffles with Joseph Smith had soured Sarah toward the Church, something of which her husband seemed at least mostly unaware. So while Orson Sr. was blissfully off on his mission, Sarah embarked on a mission all her own: to actively turn her children against Mormonism. It was a mission fraught with difficulty: she had to clandestinely hide what she was doing from Church authorities, her neighbors, and even her husband. But Sarah had mad skills.

In an interview with the *New York Herald* on May 18, 1877, she later explained the difficulty of what she had to do: "Fortunately my husband was almost constantly absent on foreign missions. I had not only to prevent my children from being Mormons, I had to see to it that they should not become imbued with such an early prejudice as would cause them to betray to the neighbors my teachings and intentions."

How on earth did she accomplish such a thing? Since inquiring minds undoubtedly wanted to know, she spilled the whole thing to the *New York Herald* reporter:

> Many a night, when my children were young and also when they had grown up so as to be companions to me, I have closed this very room where we are sitting, locked the door, pulled down the window curtains, put out all but one candle on the table, gathered my boys close around my chair and talked to them in whispers for fear that what I said would be overheard.[7]

Yikes! Shut the curtains and whispered by the dim glow of a single candle? Imagine what an impression *that* must have made on young Orson Jr., who was especially close to his mother. But he wasn't the only one: of Sarah's six children who reached adulthood, only one remained a practicing Mormon—her deaf son, Laron (who obviously couldn't hear her efforts to dissuade the bunch).

Sarah's nighttime firesides ended up having a significant effect on her children. Her youngest son, Arthur, pretty much summed up the family's feelings in 1882 when he told a newspaper reporter, "I will tell you why [I am not a Mormon]. I am the son of my father's first wife, and had a mother who taught me the evils of the system."[8]

Amazingly, the family's apostasy was carefully kept under wraps for almost twenty years. In fact, it was not until the spring of 1864 that one of them first openly announced his disbelief in Mormonism. And that intrepid chap was none other than our hero, Orson Pratt Jr.

But a *lot* of water went under the bridge before that shocking announcement was made, and for all intents and purposes, Orson Jr. *seemed* to be numbered solidly among the faithful. He even used his musical talents and education to further the cause of Zion.

Orson Pratt Sr., serving another mission in England, announced his son's marriage in the December 6, 1856, *Millennial Star*:

> Married, in Great Salt Lake City . . . Mr. Orson Pratt, Junior, to Miss Susan Snow, daughter of Zerubabel Snow, formerly a United States' Judge for that Territory. Ceremony by President Brigham Young . . . the 1st of October, 1856. The age of the bridegroom is about 19 years, that of the bride about 15. May the God of our ancestor Joseph, who was sold into Egypt, bless them, and their generations after them, for ever and ever.[9]

At that point, at least, it *seemed* that Orson Jr. was still a believing member of the Church. The evidence was certainly there. He bore his testimony in the April 1857 general conference, for one thing.[10] For another, he played the Tabernacle organ in a private conference for Church leaders that was attended by Brigham Young, Daniel Wells, George A. Smith, and Amasa Lyman.[11] The same year he was appointed to the Utah Board of Regents, he was ordained a high priest; on October 16, 1859, he was set apart as a Salt Lake Stake high councilman.

Sounds like a card-carrying member of the Church, right?

Not so, Orson Jr. later said. In that later announcement, he testified that he had done all that while he was an "unbeliever."

What on earth?

Why would someone who no longer believed accept a call as a high councilman? True, the whole gang of Pratts was keeping quiet about their apostasy at the time, but it still begs the question why Orson Jr. would accept such a calling absent a testimony of the truthfulness of the gospel. There could be a number of reasons. Maybe he felt intimidated or pressured; after all, he was only twenty-two. Maybe he thought it was easier just to accept the call than to say no—and then have to explain why not. Maybe he thought his testimony would grow if he fulfilled the calling. Or maybe, like his unbelieving mother, he simply felt an "earnest, conscientious desire to do what was right as a Mormon."[12] (If that's really how Sarah felt, she had a funny way of showing it.)

Late the next year, in October 1860, Orson Jr. left his teaching position in Salt Lake and relocated to St. George as part of a family mission call to establish a cotton industry in Southern Utah. The American Civil War was creating a cotton shortage across the nation, and Brigham Young sent men from all walks of life to what became known as "the cotton mission." Orson Sr. was called with Erastus Snow to co-preside over the whole affair.

Orson Jr. had limited resources; he and his young bride lived in a tent. Seriously. A tent. Nonetheless, he was elected a city alderman and became the area's first postmaster. He continued his musical career, playing for church and other functions on an organ his mother (still hiding her own apostasy) had hauled from Salt Lake. He and a group of friends formed a debate club that met often in his tent. Finally, he, his sister Celestia, and her husband, Albert, were also active in a local theatre troupe.

Clearly, Orson Jr. had a lot of demands on his time in addition to cultivating cotton. And that's only one reason it's so surprising that on May 2 he was ordained a high councilman of the Southern Utah Mission by his father—who was apparently unaware that his son no longer believed the Church was true. You got it: for a *second* time, Orson Jr. threw caution to the wind and accepted a call as a high councilman with his testimony missing in action.

But hang on—this story gets odder by the minute. Even though he was already up to his eyeballs in the cotton mission, Orson Jr. received a call in the spring of 1863 from Brigham Young to serve a full-time mission elsewhere.

Orson Jr., who could no longer keep up the charade, told Brigham Young he had experienced a change in his religious feelings and did not want to serve a mission.

Brigham Young insisted.

Orson Jr., equally insistent, said no.

Brigham Young counseled with Orson Jr., received a shaky agreement on Orson Jr.'s part to go, and returned to Salt Lake, thinking he'd had the final word.

He hadn't.

On June 13, 1863, Orson Jr. clarified his previously firm stand against serving a mission and sealed the deal by writing the following letter to the prophet Brigham Young:

> During your recent visit to Saint George, I informed you of the change that had taken place in my religious views, thinking that, in such a case, you would not insist on my undertaking the mission assigned me. You received me kindly and gave me what I have no doubt you considered good fatherly advice. I was much affected during the interview and hastily made a promise which, subsequent reflection commences me it is not my duty to perform. I trust that you are

well enough acquainted with my character to
know that I am actuated by none but the purest
motives. I am grateful for the interest you have
manifested in my welfare and desire still to re-
tain your friendship. Should any thing hereafter
occur to convince me that my present decision is
unwise I shall be ready to revoke it.

Imagine, if you will the look, on Brigham Young's face when
he received the letter. After all, if you refused a mission call in the
nineteenth century—unless special circumstances prevailed—you
might as well have taken out a billboard and announced your
personal apostasy. (Just a few years earlier, President Heber C.
Kimball of the First Presidency had said that unless a man "has a
just and honorable reason for not going [when he has been called],
if he does not go he will be severed from the Church."[13]) And you
know what *that* means.

But that was that. Orson Jr. was serious. He had drawn his
line in the sand.

And, much to Brigham Young's credit, he merely set the letter
aside. He did not insist that any action be taken against Orson Jr.
Truth be told, he probably hoped it was just a phase the young
man was going through. You know how *that* is.

But it wasn't just a phase.

The next year, on May 8, 1864, Orson Jr. resigned from the St.
George High Council. His father was on his way to serve a mission
in Austria, so he wasn't around to hear the resignation. Apostle
Erastus Snow—Orson Jr.'s uncle by marriage—*was* there. He was
intensely displeased but accepted the resignation, saying he could
not refuse Orson Jr.'s "liberty to withdraw from the Council"
since he had made clear he doubted "the divinity of the call of
the Prophet Joseph Smith and the consequent building up of the
Church." It was a fancy (and accurate) way of saying that Orson Jr.
no longer believed the Church was true.

Orson Jr. now had some time on his hands, but he didn't stay
idle for long. Just a week after resigning from the high council,

he and three friends published the first issue of a semi-monthly manuscript newspaper, the *Veprecula*. The first issue contained an essay by Orson Jr., writing under the pen name *Veritas* (truth) on reason and faith—the exact issue with which he was struggling.

Once Orson Jr. came out of the closet as an unbeliever, it was impossible for him to continue living in St. George. He blamed most of his difficulties on Erastus Snow, whom he publicly called a "snake in the grass." In a public speech on September 18, 1864, he blamed Snow for not only working against Orson Sr. until he drove his father away to a distant mission, but said the Apostle had secretly met with his wife, Susan, trying to turn her against Orson Jr.[14]

It hadn't worked. Susan stayed loyal to her husband.

On September 1, 1864, Susan gave birth to the couple's first child, Arthur Eugene. Just seventeen days later, the family's difficulties with Mormonism came to a head. Orson Jr.'s doubts were no longer under wraps; after all, he had resigned from the high council. While Brigham Young stayed mute on the matter, the local authorities felt obligated to convene a Church court.

On September 18, 1864, Orson Jr. was given the unusual opportunity of defending himself in the glaringly public setting of sacrament meeting. The twenty-seven-year-old took the stand and made his shocking announcement:

> I wish to say that I have long since seen differently to this people and although I am not in the habit of saying anything in self justification, yet ever since I have been in this Church I have led a godly and upright life; at the same time, I resolved that I would accept nothing that my conscience would not receive. I was at eight years old, baptized into the Church, and I was brought up in the Church. Well if I had been asked at that time what I was baptized for, I should have said for the remission of my sins, for I had learned it all parrot like and I

had confidence in Mormonism, as I had been brought up in it. . . . I came out again to the Valleys with my father and we were required to be baptized again, I complied, for all this time I was a believer in Mormonism. But sometime afterwards, there was much said . . . that unless one had the testimony that Mormonism is true, there was something deficient. I asked myself the question, if I had it but was sensible I had not. . . . I have come to the conclusion that Joseph Smith was not specially sent by the Lord to establish this work, and I cannot help it, for I could not believe otherwise, even if I knew that I was to be punished for not doing so; and I must say so though I knew that I was to suffer for it the next moment.[15]

The shock was not that Orson no longer believed. The shock was that he had done so much—received his endowment, born testimony in general conference, served on two high councils, and accepted a mission call to the cotton mission—all in an attitude of unbelief. It was a pretty impressive resume for someone who had completely lost his testimony.

He had kept it well hidden—some might argue he'd kept it hidden even from himself. But his address in sacrament meeting did it. Orson Pratt Jr. was excommunicated that night for "unbelief" by the St. George High Council, of which he had until recently served as a member.

Within a few days, the entire Pratt family pulled up stakes and started the northward trek back to home and hearth in Salt Lake. Orson Jr. and Susan went on to have three more children, giving them two sons and two daughters.

Orson Sr. continued his missionary service, being absent for long stretches of time. Orson Jr. and Susan lived with his mother, Sarah, for more than a decade. Even after she sold her home in 1881, she occasionally lived with them as well as with her other children. After years of suffering with a heart condition, she died on Christmas Day, 1889.

While he never reconciled with the Church, Orson Jr. became, as his obituary put it, one of the "foremost musicians" of Salt Lake City.[16] He taught music, art, and literature, and became known as one of the most successful and prominent teachers in the state.

By the turn of the century, Orson Jr.'s health began to deteriorate. Evidently, his mother's impact on his heart went way beyond poisoning him against Mormonism: he and all his siblings inherited his mother's cardiovascular disease, and all suffered relatively early deaths as a result. Orson Jr. actually lived longer than any of them.

With his health in precarious condition as the year 1903 drew to a close, he went north to Ogden to stay with his son Arthur, hoping a change of scenery would help. It didn't. He died on December 6, 1903, at Arthur's home at the age of sixty-seven. He was remembered at a small, private funeral and was buried in the Salt Lake City Cemetery.

Susan Lizette Snow Pratt outlived her husband by twenty-four years, dying at the home of her daughter on May 16, 1927. She is buried next to her husband. Her obituary is brief, making no mention of the Church other than to say she arrived in Salt Lake with pioneers when she was nine. One is left to assume she never renewed her fellowship with the Saints.

George Armstrong Hicks's backbreaking work in the "Cotton Mission" led him to write his ballad, "Once I Lived in Cottonwood"—not amusing to Church leaders, but a wildly popular favorite of local members.

GEORGE ARMSTRONG HICKS
SPEAKING OUT OF BOTH SIDES OF HIS MOUTH

THEY SAY BEAUTY IS ONLY skin deep—and in the case of George Armstrong Hicks, you might say that what you see on the surface isn't *at all* what you get below that. You see, on the surface, George appeared to be what historian Davis Bitton called "a typical Mormon pioneer . . . raised in the Church, crossing the plains in 1852, answering the call to colonize remote areas of Utah Territory, and dying in the faith as an old man."[1]

That was on the *surface*.

Probe a little deeper, and you get one of the most colorful and fascinating characters in Church history—a guy who seemed to be with it but who was plagued by doubts about Church leadership and doctrine; who "wrote impudent letters to Brigham Young; alienated the testy Emma Lee, who threatened to 'put a load of salt in his backside'; and may even have been excommunicated for a time."[2]

Make that two times.[3] The first was when he questioned why John D. Lee was still a Mormon in good standing a decade after the massacre at Mountain Meadows. (It was a bit easier to get excommunicated back then.) The second time occurred in about 1884 when he wrote his bishop that Utah would never become a state until the Mormons gave up polygamy.

That offended the bishop, who was a polygamist.

Apparently it was a *lot* easier to get excommunicated back then. (Even when, as was apparently the case with George Armstrong Hicks, you were a man ahead of your time.)

More about both of those excommunications later.

Lucky for us, we have a detailed, candid, and humorous autobiography penned in 1878 by George Armstrong Hicks himself at the age of forty-three—a literary tome that gives us remarkable insight into what was going on in that head of his. By 1878, he had, shall we say, become a little bitter. *Alienated* is the word that's often used. Even so, it's possible to see much faith and insight in his writing. As Bitton reminds us, George was not "one of the leaders, whose perspective often shaped the writing of history, but one of the 'toilers,' one of the 'hewers of wood and drawers of water.'"4

This is a man who "provides a valuable point of view. Too often we lump the people of territorial Utah into two large categories—Mormons and gentiles—the former portrayed as all devout, the latter as vehement persecutors. . . . Hicks is a fascinating example of a Mormon who positioned himself close to the edge, just inside or just outside the boundary."5

And his life is one that will probably leave you shaking your head with amusement at a complex character stuffed to the brim with eccentricities.

You also get a guy who waxed poetic on occasion—especially on rough occasions. When he was called by Brigham Young to the "cotton mission," an agricultural experiment in Southern Utah to help supplement cotton stores that had been depleted by the Civil War, he obeyed. He worked his heart out. And he pretty much hated it. Putting his lyrics to a common folk song, he composed "Once I Lived in Cottonwood." Church leaders couldn't have been too amused, but it's a song that's still sung today.

For now, let's start at the beginning. George Armstrong Hicks was born January 14, 1835, near Toronto, Canada, the oldest son of George Barton and Martha Ann Wilson Hicks. When George was just two years old, Theodore Turley—a former mechanic, gunsmith, brewer, farmer, blacksmith, gristmill operator, and Methodist-turned-Mormon-missionary—swept through town, bringing the message of the restored gospel. And Turley wasn't alone: other missionaries who came to the area included Almon W. Babbitt and the Prophet Joseph Smith himself, who testified of receiving and translating the Book of Mormon.

That did it. George Barton Hicks, his wife, his parents, and four of his brothers entered the waters of baptism. Two-year-old George may not have remembered his parents' conversion, but he undoubtedly heard about it often enough throughout the rest of their lives. And as a result, of course, he was raised in the Church.

When George was just three, the Hicks family left Canada—something George said he remembered[6]—and started out for Jackson County, Missouri. Instead of going straight through to Missouri, they stopped for the summer to earn the cash that would take them the rest of the way. Setting up camp in Georgetown, Pennsylvania, George found a job as a weaver, and Martha opened a confectionary shop.

That was a lucky turn of events: while George and Martha were slaving away in Pennsylvania, Missouri Governor Lilburn Boggs issued the infamous Extermination Order, driving the Saints out of Missouri under brutal conditions. George and Martha stayed put until it looked like things had settled down for the Mormons; when they finally left Pennsylvania, it wasn't for Missouri but for Commerce, which would become Nauvoo, Illinois. They arrived in November 1839.

Obviously, George was too young to remember much about the early years in Nauvoo, but he clearly drew on family lore to fill in the blanks in his autobiography. That first winter in Nauvoo, even for a hardy group of folks used to the Canadian winters, was "severe," he wrote. His family lived in a "rude" log cabin that had no window or floor. The next spring, 1840, his father built a better log house.

Things seemed to be booming in Nauvoo—the population was soaring, construction was flourishing, and gardens and orchards were being planted. There were just two problems, and they were pretty serious: Nauvoo was built on a swamp, and hordes of people were ill with a malaria-like sickness. Some died. The other problem was an economic one: most people had little or no money. If they did, they weren't convinced they should invest it in Nauvoo—after all, the Mormons hadn't had much sticking power up to that point.

There were schools in Nauvoo, George remembered, but they were private, and there was tuition that had to be paid. Nauvoo, George reflected, was "a hard place for the poor to make a living in"; without the spare cash to pay a teacher, his parents couldn't afford to send George to school. As a result, Martha taught her children at home. There were three books in the Hicks house at the time: the Bible, the Book of Mormon, and *Voice of Warning* by Parley P. Pratt.

Martha told George she'd buy him his own copy of the Book of Mormon if he would read it. He promised. She bought him the book. Right away, he got caught up in the wars between the Nephites and the Lamanites—"but before I got through," he wrote, "the book fell into a tub of soap suds and was spoiled, so I did not read it through."[7]

While George never really got back into the Book of Mormon—and certainly not into the doctrines or religious messages—he loved to read Pratt's *Voice of Warning*. His attitude about it in 1878 demonstrates the slippery slope on which his faith had careened:

> I think it is one of the finest religious books I ever read. It is a great pity that it is not true. [Referring to the little stone cut from the mountain without hands and shattering the great image,] I asked my mother when these things should take place. She told me that the "little stone" is the Mormon Church and that the time for breaking the "Image" is now—in a few years. That was the faith of the whole Mormon Church and my parents were not to

blame for believing it. Over thirty years have
passed and gone yet the "Image" is still standing and the "Stone" is showing signs of decay.[8]

George didn't like polygamy—not while he was in Nauvoo and
not almost four decades later when he penned his autobiography.
In fact, it was one of the great aversions of this life. At that
point, he claimed it was *the* cause of the deaths of Joseph and
Hyrum Smith. He even went so far as to call it the "rock" that
the Church "came near splitting upon in the days of Nauvoo." It's
pretty easy to see where he developed such a view: between the
time he was eight and ten, Elizabeth Brewerton—one of Parley
P. Pratt's wives—moved in with the Hicks family. And so it was
that George watched Parley come to visit. *That* has to have been
a bit awkward.

But listen to this: despite his bold statement that polygamy
"is and always was disagreeable to the female member of the
church," the perplexed reader notices this a few lines later: "I as
an individual have no particular objections to polygamy. [*What?*]
I know the laws of nature allow the practice of it and if people of
mature judgment wish to practice it I have no objections."[9] Oh,
my. Just wait and see what happened later.

Those aren't the only inconsistencies in Hicks's account. He
speaks glowingly of both Joseph Smith and Brigham Young, then
before you can catch your breath tromps on both for a host of
character flaws—many, he admits, based on hearsay. It's almost
like a one-way trip through the Twilight Zone. After bashing both
the Prophet and Brigham Young, George relates that his father was
at the meeting on August 8, 1844, when the mantle of Joseph fell
on his successor, Brigham Young. George's response? "I believe it, I
believe the spirit of Joseph took possession of the body of Brigham
and spoke to the people through him. Brigham was the man to
take the lead."[10]

We guess, for George Armstrong Hicks, you *can* have it both
ways.

Even though he was still a child, George witnessed firsthand
the persecution and the dissension that marked the Nauvoo days.

By the time he wrote his autobiography, he blamed the Church itself for the persecution it suffered, going so far as to say that he blamed Orrin Porter Rockwell for the assassination attempt on Lilburn Boggs in 1842. The only reason he failed, George theorized, was that he put two balls in the gun and that he shot at Boggs through a glass window.

George also witnessed firsthand the result of discord in Nauvoo: when he was only nine, George's elderly grandmother and four of his uncles became followers of William Law, who had come out in opposition to Joseph Smith. Law, who had been a member of the First Presidency under Joseph Smith, was excommunicated and subsequently formed his own church, the True Church of Jesus Christ of Latter Day Saints. While it attracted a fair amount of followers, it lasted about as long as custard when it's left out of the refrigerator.

George's parents stayed true to Joseph Smith, but also respected family ties. When George's uncle Samuel Hicks was burned out of his home at Camp Creek, George and Martha invited Samuel's family to move in with them on the farm they rented outside Nauvoo, even though Samuel and his family had followed Law.

That's when creepy stuff started happening. Chickens got stolen from the farm—all the time. And one time, when George was ten, a huge hog was stolen in the middle of the night. The next day, George's father and uncle tracked the parties to Nauvoo, "but they did not recover the pork." Reflecting on the vandalism and theft that took place on the farm, George wrote, "I presume that many in Nauvoo thought that because my father's folks had most of them left the church and we were living on land that belonged to a gentile, we were no better than apostates and it was no harm to rob us before we followed the Laws [William Laws's church] to Wisconsin."[11]

Young George Hicks and his family left Nauvoo with the body of the Saints in 1846, when George was eleven. His father sold two log houses—one of them filled to the rafters with un-threshed wheat—for "the paltry sum of four dollars," George remembered. "It was all he could get and that was more than some got for better places than ours. He took the money, and we gave up our home. It was a humble one, it is true, but it was our own and all we had."

George opined that the expulsion of the Mormons from Nauvoo was cruel. No argument there—most thinking people couldn't agree more. But by 1878, he blamed *the Mormons* for that expulsion. Yes, you read right. They should have been tougher, he said, writing, "If the Mormons had have punished offenders among themselves and used due diligence to assist officers of the law to catch all who were transgressors against the law we might have been living in Hancock County today and have been at peace with all mankind, but it was otherwise to be."[12]

Maybe he was remembering that big, fat hog some supposed Mormons stole from the farm.

On their way out of Nauvoo, the Hicks family had one yoke of cattle but no wagon for the cattle to tow. George's father "got use of a wagon" from a fellow Saint named Whitford Wilson. It's not clear exactly what that means—whether he borrowed it, was given it, or bought it. Maybe that's how he used the proceeds from the sale of his two houses. We guess it doesn't matter much, because as you'll see in a minute, the Hicks family didn't make the traditional beeline for the Beehive State.

Eleven-year-old George and his family "crossed the big river and went not knowing whether we went into a strange land among strangers." It was a long and winding road for them, and George remembered a lot of not-so-positive aspects of the journey. So it can only be counted as another of his bizarre inconsistencies when he wrote in his autobiography:

> As I look back upon those scenes, I think we must have been inspired with something more than common zeal. There was, it seemed, a power behind the scene invisible to us that prodded us to "go" and, to use one of the sayings of George A. Smith, we went cheerfully when we were obliged to. There was a vast territory in the West that was waiting for the hand of

industry to bring it into usefulness, and Providence had decreed that we, the Mormon exiles who could not live in peace with the people of Missouri and Illinois must go and build up— shall I say an empire?—no, we must be purified in the wilderness. We must live alone and learn to live on our own resources, and to prepare the way for the spread of the great republic of the West. We did not realize the greatness of our mission at that time, but as a panorama of the years have rolled by, these things have been made manifest. The individual must be blind indeed who cannot see that there has been a power that has guided the destiny of the Mormon people. We had a work to do, and it seems as though it is done.

As we said a minute ago, the Hicks family did not take the direct and unfettered route to Utah. Like Moses and the children of Israel who took what has to be the longest and most painful route possible to the promised land, the Hicks family made an eight-year hiatus out of the trip, living in either Iowa or Nebraska while the rest of the pioneers zoomed by on their way to Zion.

Their first stop was in Bonaparte, Iowa, a small town on the shores of the Des Moines River. They had gone an astonishing thirty-five miles since leaving Nauvoo. George's father—and, to be fair, a bunch of other men—found jobs in Bonaparte, as the farmers were just beginning to harvest their crops. The pay was fair, too, since the farmers were willing to pay just about anything to get their crops out of the ground.

Looked good to George's father. So they parked their wagon— you remember, the one they "got use of"—and set up camp.

Fast-forward a few weeks . . . George's father was laboring in the fields when he was overcome by one of the most dread diseases of the day: cholera. A couple of the other farm hands carried him home, and they sent for Dr. Wyman—a man young

George referred to as "an infidel." Fancy way of saying he wasn't a Mormon (or a believer of any other faith, for that matter).

Dr. Wyman arrived at the house they were renting, administered medication, and sat by his patient's bedside. His usual charge was one dollar per visit, a hefty sum when you consider that was the monthly rent on an apartment back then.

Cholera was a deadly disease, and by the time all was said and done, Dr. Wyman had made *seven* trips to the house to mete out treatment to his suffering patient. One can only imagine the financial stress the Hicks family felt each time the good doctor burst through the door.

When he had finally recovered, George Hicks mustered up his courage and asked the doctor for his bill. Dr. Wyman rubbed his chin, assessed the situation, and responded, "Hicks if you will haul me a [expletive deleted] good load of wood I will be satisfied."

It was a humbling experience for George, as it was for the entire family. The doctor may have labeled himself an infidel, but young George considered him a Christian, "for he 'visited the sick' and 'did unto others as he would have had them do unto him.' His heart was warm and kind and he knew how to sympathize with the poor and he felt it was his duty to administer to their sufferings. I am sorry there is not more such 'infidels' in the world."[13]

By June 1847, the Mormons had decided to "gather up to Headquarters," which at the time was Council Bluffs, Iowa. The Hicks weren't about to be left out, so they gathered up their few belongings and started out, probably in the same wagon they had "got use of" earlier.

We're sure you won't be surprised to learn that there were some . . . um, distractions along the way. After a few weeks of travel by ox and wagon, the Hicks family arrived at the east bank of the Missouri River. There they encountered a group of Saints who "had an abundance of corn and buckwheat and seemed as happy as though they had never been driven from their homes. They seemed to 'take joyfully to the spoiling of their goods.'"

The older George Hicks, who liked what he saw, deemed it a great place for his family. He parked the wagon and declared that there they would stay. But by the end of the summer he had other ideas, and moved his family to Bullocks Grove to spend the winter. To be fair, they were in the "area" of Council Bluffs, so it was legit.

At Bullocks Grove, the family lived in a log house in the woods, isolated from schools and meetinghouses. George remembers that they were "comparatively happy," since they had good health. And he enjoyed a bit of adventure as well: the woods were full of "prairie chickens"—large brown-, black-, and white-feathered grouse—and he made great sport of catching them in traps.

As it turned out, the Hicks family ended up spending five years in the area. That spring, they fenced off a small farm a mile or so north of Kanesville, Iowa, where they grew "an abundance" of corn, potatoes, and buckwheat. They also built a log cabin on the property, where they found themselves living among a number of their old neighbors from Nauvoo (seems they weren't the only ones who took their time crossing the plains). George wrote that "many was the social gathering at our houses. Long winter months were passed in dancing and religious exercises, for the 'Latter-day Saints' were full of brotherly love and faith in the future, triumphing in the gospel dispensation."

Things were not all sunshine and roses for poor teenaged George, though: every year, pretty much like clockwork, he was leveled by "fever and ague" for weeks at a time. On two different occasions he started school with a teacher, but he didn't continue for more than a few weeks because of illness.

His father, not wanting to see George's mind rot, brought him lots of books to read while he languished in bed. Teenaged George was picky about what he read, though: books about religious doctrine and theory bored him to tears, so his father indulged him by providing him romance and adventure volumes.

During the winter of 1851–1852, most of the Saints in Council Bluffs started rumbling about setting out for Utah the next summer. George Hicks was no exception; it was time for his family to head for Utah (eight years late, but, hey, what's a few years?), so he started making preparations in earnest. As for young George, he considered the time on the farm as a place "where we had toiled for five years preparing for the journey." He mentioned in his autobiography one ox team and a couple of cows, along with "great faith." And we imagine they had a wagon, though maybe not the same one they "got use of" eight years earlier. Eight years is a long time.

Young George mentioned that they sold their home for a "song," and on June 5, 1852, they set out on their way to Utah. Of the trip, he wrote:

> We believed we were of the chosen of God, that it was our duty to gather out of Babylon while the judgments of God should pass over the nation. It has been so for the great rebellion [the Civil War] in the U.S. Which has cost the Nation so much blood and treasure, has "passed over" the country. I think I am safe in saying that Utah has suffered the least of any state or territory in the Union by the war. It would be very hard for me to believe that the gathering of the Mormon people was all the work of chance and fanaticism. There is divinity (I think).

I think? Gotta love his conviction. As Bitton wrote, "In these few lines we find a complex mix: recollections of the buoyant spirit of the gathering and of predictions about the United States; a boastful claim that the prophecy had been fulfilled; and . . . a reluctant, tentative acknowledgment of divine guidance of the Mormon westward movement."[14]

The group with which the Hickses traveled followed the typical Mormon pattern. The group was organized into companies of fifty wagons, with a captain appointed over each company; the Hicks family was led by Captain Walker. Each company of fifty was further divided into companies of ten, with a captain over each ten wagons; George and his family were in the fourteenth company, headed by John Myres. On the last day of June, the company crossed the Missouri River at Winter Quarters and, wrote George, "bid farewell to the United States."

The trip was not a pleasant one.

Before they had traveled far, cholera broke out among the pioneers; thirteen in George's company died of the disease. George's brother Moroni was the first to get sick, but like his father before him, he recovered. George noted that he "saw the ordinance of laying on of hands tried to no purpose."

"It was sad to part with loved ones and leave them forever on the lonely plains to return to dust," he wrote. "We hurried along as fast as our ox teams could be made to travel so that we could get out of the stricken district. . . . The way was marked by graves more frequent than mile stones in the old states."

For a teenager, it had to be rough going. George wrote, "It was generally young people and women who died on the plains. I remember helping to bury one woman on the plains who was still warm. We had no coffins, but used the bark off the cottonwood trees when it could be obtained."

The staple diet for the pioneers was buffalo, and the hunt for them was high adventure for George, who killed one himself. They saw huge herds of the animals as well as many peaceable Sioux Indians. As they climbed in altitude, the cholera gradually subsided.

On October 3, 1852, they reached Salt Lake City. At last their journey was over—almost. George wrote:

> On the 3rd day of October, 1852, we arrived in Great Salt Lake City all in good health but very much worn by our long and weary journey of 1,030 miles. We were within two days of being 4 months from the time we left our home in Potawatamie County, Iowa until we reached the end of our journey and the rest was sweet.
>
> We were met at one of the public squares by old friends and kindly welcomed. One friend,

Jonathan Packer by name, invited our whole ten to his house in one of the lower wards where he had a large and splendid garden of choice vegetables. He invited us in and bid us help ourselves to such as we liked best, and be assured, we feasted on the fine potatoes, squashes and cabbages. This was certainly brotherly.

Utah had been settled by five years before we came in and Salt Lake City was a mere village at that time, but the Saints had done wonders considering their circumstances. They had plenty of the common necessaries of life. Wheat was worth $2.00 per bushel and flour $6.00 per 100 pounds. My father had brought 400 lbs of salaratus from the alkali lakes on the plains and this he sold for 25 cents per pound in flour and vegetables.

The Hicks family temporarily stayed at what was called the "Big Field," a common grazing area where many incoming pioneers camped until they figured out what to do next. It didn't take George Hicks long to figure out what he was going to do: once the October general conference of 1852 was over, a matter of only a few days, he rounded up his weary party and headed to Palmyra, a new settlement just being established on the Spanish Fork River.

If anyone in the family expected luxurious digs, they were sorely disappointed. The family spent the winter in a dugout, "made by digging a celler [*sic*] or hole in the ground and putting a roof of willows and earth over it and then making a fireplace inside."[15] George remembered that many of the Saints who had crossed the plains that summer settled in Palmyra. They were, he wrote, "poor in worlds goods, but they were full of hope for the future and faith in the gospel which they had received, and when we made a move, there was united effort."

Sounds like young George liked Palmyra. In fact, he did. And one of the reasons was the Henry Bryant Jolley family—especially their fifteen-year-old daughter, Elizabeth. They attended school together that winter, and George did well. "I was a student in the school of Mr. [Silas] Hillman, and graduated at the end of the first quarter with 'high honors,'" George wrote, "being able to read in the Testament or the Book of Mormon without making many mistakes in the Pronounciation [*sic*] of words; with a very limited knowledge of arithmetic and none whatever of grammar or history."[16]

As the year progressed, however, George focused more on Elizabeth than on his studies; he later wrote, "I fear there was more love making than studying of books, for young lovers make bad students of books."[17] The next spring, the pair was married. George had just turned eighteen.

Life in early Palmyra was colorful all on its own. There were more than a few clashes with Indians; George participated in the militia in some of them, served as an interpreter in some of the negotiations, and even smoked a peace pipe with one group of Indian leaders. That must have made the theft of the hog look like child's play.

Then there were the grasshoppers. Salt Lake had its crickets, and Palmyra had its grasshoppers. What seemed like millions of them. In the spring of 1854, what George described as "a shower of grasshoppers" descended on the crops. That was bad enough. The next spring, the millions of eggs deposited the previous year hatched, and most of the grain was destroyed. Everything that was green (other than some large box elder trees) was devoured. Remembering the devastation in 1878, George blamed Brigham Young—after all, he should have told them how to fight the grasshoppers, he reasoned. Instead, the prophet "told us that the grasshoppers were the Lord's army and that God's judgments must commence at the house of God and we believed him correct. The blind lead the blind and we all fell into the ditch together."[18]

As if the grasshopper disaster hadn't been enough, George Hicks took what he interpreted to be a series of sucker punches to his faith in 1856.

The first—and we have to admit this would have been a bitter pill to swallow—came when the settlers in Palmyra discovered that the irrigation caused alkali to rise to the surface. Alkaline soil equals wrecked crops. The only possible solution was obvious: get away from that alkaline soil. In fact, Brigham Young "told the people of Palmyra their settlement was poorly located and instructed them to move to Spanish Fork."[19]

George didn't fault Brigham Young. In fact, the prophet was right, he felt.

Instead, the man who got George's wrath was Elder George A. Smith, whom he called the "inspired idiot" originally responsible for selecting Palmyra as a settlement. Elder Smith, speaking in the schoolhouse, had promised that "greatness" was in store for the citizens of Palmyra, and they had believed him. In fact, George himself had "thanked God that we had an inspired priesthood that could tell us the future while the gentiles had to grovel in darkness."[20]

That was before the alkali problem reared its ugly head. By then, George had abruptly changed his tune, writing in his 1878 autobiography that those who had listened to "the 'inspired' raving of the 'man of God' had the 'satisfaction' of losing all their buildings, for water began to raise in the cellars of the houses and we must move and lose nearly two years work. I lost a house that cost me $300 in hard labor and I never lived in it an hour."[21]

It was a devastating blow that stayed with him for years. In 1913 "he wrote more fully of the sandy loam that made Palmyra undesirable for farming, the efforts of the settlers to obtain permission to relocate, George A. Smith's adamant refusal, and Brigham Young's wise approval."[22] While some of the finer details were reported a bit differently, it's easy to see that George was still smarting almost six decades later when he wrote, "Four long trying years we worked there under trying circumstances. All the improvements we had made in those four years in the form of homes was a total loss, and all because we had listened to bad advice. The writer of this essay had just finished putting on the roof of a house in the fort when the counsel came from headquarters to leave Palmyra. That house cost two hundred and fifty dollars in labor, I having hauled rock from the mountains for a foundation."[23]

The other event of 1856 that profoundly impacted George's faith was the doom of the ill-fated Martin Handcart Company. For whatever reason, he focused on the Martin Company, even though the Willie Company also suffered. Again, he blamed Church leaders, who, as George wrote, "prophesied that the Lord would turn the storms to the right hand and the left and that they should be brought through the mountains like the children of Israel were brought through the Red Sea." Never mind that the two handcart companies got off to a disastrously late start. Never mind that Church leaders strongly advised them against trying to make the trip, counseling them to wait until the next summer. And never mind that it was the members of the handcart companies themselves who insisted on tallying-ho.

Never mind all that because George was fixated on Church leaders as being at fault. The catastrophic experience of the hand-cart companies, more than anything else, he wrote, had the effect of "completely revolutionizing" his mind:

> At that time I believed that the universe was governed by the will of a supreme being and that he kept the whole human family under his eye as it were and meted out to all according to their needs as a good father would do for his children and "that the righteous were never forsaken." These poor hand cart companies called upon God twice every day; they sang psalms to his praise as they traveled along; they hoped; they trusted in him but all in vain. I do not believe that "God" will ever have a better opertunity [sic] to help our suffering humanity than then. The truth is the universe is governed by laws immutable and unchangeable.[24]

George was, plain and simple, unforgiving in dishing out the blame for the disaster. And this time, it was two-fold. "Those poor people were not lost because they were either good or bad," he wrote, "but because they were the unfortunate victims of the Church leader's mistakes."[25] But that wasn't the end of it: according to George, "God had simply not come through in the clutches."[26]

Harsh.

And that wasn't the end of it. George suffered further blows to his faith from the Mormon War of 1857–1858 (which Bitton described as "a series of episodes that in retrospect seem at times to be from a Gilbert and Sullivan farce"[27]). And then there was the Mountain Meadows Massacre. As Bitton observed, "Totally incompetent as a witness to the massacre himself—he was nowhere near the scene—Hicks characteristically blamed the Church authorities, specifically Brigham Young."[28]

Now you have a good idea how George Armstrong Hicks was feeling—about Church leaders, about the Church itself, and about life in general—which makes what happened next all the more puzzling.

In 1861, George moved with his family to Pond Town—present-day Salem, in Utah County. It was a convenient move if there ever was one: George's father-in-law, Henry Bryant Jolley, was the bishop there. *Still a devout member of the Church*—if you can believe it, given his attitudes during the previous decade or so—George was hoping to get a recommend. He wanted more than anything to be sealed to his wife in the Endowment House.

But before that could happen, something else did: George was called to go to Southern Utah and settle in the Dixie Mission. It was a call that included not only George, but Bishop Jolley and all of his other sons-in-law as well.

Remember, this is George Armstrong Hicks, a guy who didn't have the best of attitudes toward Church leaders . . . especially Brigham Young. But, oddly enough, he jumped on board with the plan to go to Dixie as soon as Brigham Young asked. He sold his property for about half what he had paid for it just a few months earlier and headed south in late November. He later confessed to having a "heavy heart" even before the group pulled out of Pond Town. But pull out he did.

It was a terrible journey—not the first George had endured. As Bitton writes, "The journey south-ward was no picnic. Driving cattle and sheep, the company finally reached Black Ridge and camped for the night. Unfortunately, an unusual storm brought some two feet of snow accompanied by a terrible wind of gale proportions. The draft animals wandered from camp and were not found until more than a week later."[29]

Finally, almost at their destination, the company was invited by some nearby residents to settle in Harmony. Nothing doing— Bishop Jolley insisted on carrying out his orders "to the very letter." We can only imagine what George was silently thinking at this point. Still the beleaguered group pushed on, finally arriving in Washington. George was less than thrilled with the accommodations. He wrote that the ground was "dry and dusty" and that they "were at the end of our journey in a sickly and barren land with very little to go upon."[30]

But still George pasted a smile on his face and dug in with the rest of the group. In the small settlement of Washington, things were never dull. George was able to get a lot on which he built a "wickiup" (a crude brush shelter); it was there that his wife, Betsy, gave birth to a baby boy, James W. When George asked mission president and Apostle Erastus Snow for some flour to help sustain his family, Snow soundly refused, saying he "couldn't feed everyone." Instead, he advised the settlers to plant "all the cane and cotton we could possibly manage." So of course, when the market for those crops tanked, George blamed President Snow.

In came Brigham Young to the rescue, building a cotton factory—something George admitted was a great idea, since it provided employment to the community and "proved a great benefit to Washington County." But out of the other side of his mouth, he complained about the quality of the factory and the price of its product.[31]

In the meantime, Bishop Jolley had relaxed his determined intention to carry out his calling to the very letter and had relocated to Harmony—you remember, that spot where he and his group had been invited to stop earlier. As it turned out, things didn't go too much more smoothly there. George built another wickiup, but it accidentally burned down. Needing *something* with which to support his family, he hired out as a laborer to rip up the plentiful sage by the roots; he was paid with corn. (If you've ever tried to rip sage up by the roots, especially out of dry ground, you have a feeling for what George faced.)

Thinking things were starting to look up, George obtained four acres of soil and planted it with sorghum, corn, potatoes, and other vegetables. But before he could harvest a single bite of food, a cow broke through the fence. Spying the broken fence, a herd of sheep helped themselves to the crops—all of them. By then on the edge of starvation, George had no choice but to labor for better-established settlers. Of course, he thought they took advantage of him and underpaid him.

In 1864, George vented his spleen, so to say, by writing his folk song, "Once I Lived in Cottonwood." He called it "A Ballad of Our Dixie," and intended it be sung to the tune of "Georgia Volunteer," a popular folk song of the day. In these stanzas, he recounted the call to settle Dixie, the miserable journey there, and his heartfelt feelings about the place:

> Once I lived in Cottonwood,
> And owned a little farm;
> But I was called to Dixie,
> Which did me much alarm.
>
> To raise the cane and cotton
> I right away must go,
> But the reason why they called me
> I'm sure I do not know. . . .
>
> Next we got to Washington
> Where we stayed a little while
> To see if April showers
> Would make the verdure smile.
>
> But Oh! I was mistaken,
> And so I went away,
> For the red hills of November
> Looked the same in May.

I feel so weak and lonely now,
There's nothing here to cheer
Except prophetic sermons,
Which we very often hear.

They will hand them out by dozens
And prove them by the Book;
I'd rather have some roasting ears,
To stay at home and cook.

My wagon's sold for sorghum seed,
To make a little bread.
And poor old Jim and Bolly
Long ago are dead.

There's only me and Betsy left
To hoe the cotton tree;
May heaven help the Dixieite
Wherever he may be![32]

The song became an instant hit. In fact, had there been a "top twenty" in 1864, it would have topped the charts.

Church leaders were unhappy about the popular tune, but they needn't have worried. "If the authorities feared the song would breed discontent among the hungry settlers of Dixie," writes Andrew Karl Larson, "they were mistaken. It gave them a chance to face their troubles and laugh at them." Larson feels the lyrics were "good-humored, hilarious cynicism" and "good-natured raillery."[33]

But by far the biggest challenge for George in Harmony—and yes, we saved the best for last—was the fact that his branch president was none other than John D. Lee (remember that unfortunate excommunication?). Although he admitted that Lee was an eloquent speaker and a good farmer, any respect he might have had for the man stopped there:

[George] accused Lee of misquoting scriptures,
he laughed at his faith-promoting stories, and
he branded Lee as a swindler, a liar, a sensual

brute, and a hypocrite. When Brigham Young, journeying southward on one of his tours through the settlements, stayed overnight with Lee—Lee was Young's son by adoption—Hicks was incensed.[34]

This was no mild dislike. George confronted Lee in meetings. He tried to prevent Lee from preaching. He even tried to block Lee from getting a recommend for a plural marriage.

And then there was the issue of the Mountain Meadows Massacre; George was appalled that a man who had played at least some role in the horrific incident was still a member of the Church at all, let alone a *branch president*. So on December 4, 1868, George dashed off a long, tormented letter to Brigham Young, demanding that John D. Lee be excommunicated for his involvement at Mountain Meadows.[35]

With his missive safely on its way to the Church president, George started acting . . . well, let's say lots of folks found his behavior offensive. He carried around a copy of a sermon by Brigham Young renouncing the massacre and read it loudly to anyone who would listen. He also took every opportunity to belt out a song that began with the following lyrics:

> Come all true sons of freedom, unto my rhyme give ear,
>
> It's of an awful massacre, you presently shall hear.
>
> In splendor o'er the mountains, some twenty wagons came,
>
> They were attacked by a wicked band, and Utah bears the blame.[36]

As you can imagine, George was starting to annoy his friends and neighbors. And so it was that in 1868, John D. Lee accused George of fabricating the letter. Lee ordered George out of Harmony.

It didn't stop there. One of Lee's plural wives, a strong-willed and sassy woman named Emma Lee, got in on the action as well.

She called George "a poor sneaking, pusillanimous pup, and always meddling in other men's matters." For those of you who don't know the meaning of *pusillanimous*, we'll save you a trip to the dictionary: it means cowardly, faint-hearted, and timid (not exactly adjectives we'd use to describe George). She then warned him that "he had better sing low and keep out of her path or she would put a load of salt in his backside."[37]

With that, the fight was on.

George responded by charging Emma Lee with un-Christian conduct.

They both got excommunicated, though the charges were a bit dim.

A bishop's trial was ordered, and Bishop James Pace concluded that both George and Emma Lee were wrong—but that both of them should be rebaptized.

Well, Emma Lee wasn't going to take any of it sitting down. She demanded that Bishop Pace perform the ceremony:

> Seeing that you are so inconsiderate as to require a woman to be immersed when the water is full of snow and ice, and that, too, for defending the rights of her husband, you should pay a little of the penalty for making such a decision and perhaps if your backside gets wet in the ice water, you will be more careful how you decide again.[38]

Told you she was feisty. By the way, neither George Armstrong Hicks nor Emma Lee was rebaptized that day. And we don't think it was just that the bishop didn't want to get in the ice water.

After some more back-and-forth correspondence with Brigham Young, George went on a very public campaign against the prophet and was branded an apostate.[39] But here's the weird thing: depending on the day, time, and place, he still *appeared* to be stalwart in the faith.

In 1871, he followed his parents-in-law and moved to Mount Carmel. Five years later he moved again, this time to Clinton, a sleepy little hamlet in Spanish Fork Canyon. Finally, he moved to Spanish Fork. In 1878, he started to write his now well-known autobiography. And he didn't mince words.

We wonder why George didn't just bide his time a *little* longer and even perhaps just go with the flow for a bit. After all, he seemed to be in more comfortable circumstances than he'd ever been—no more burning wickiups or ripping up sagebrush. The Church leaders he had most resented—including Brigham Young and George A. Smith—were dead. In fact, being the staunch Republican that he was, he soon found himself in alliance with a number of Church leaders, including Joseph F. Smith and Reed Smoot. And by 1890, the Woodruff Manifesto would end polygamy.

But, speaking of polygamy, George continued to get whipped up into a bigger and bigger lather about it. He just couldn't refrain from telling the Church leaders what he thought about it and what they should do, each communiqué peppered with increasingly more scathing and sarcastic comments. And that set the scene for his second excommunication.

Sometime in the 1880s, he sent a letter to his bishop in Spanish Fork, G. D. Snell, declaring in no uncertain terms that the Church should abandon polygamy. That didn't sit well with Snell, who was himself a polygamist. It also offended his sensibilities, because many polygamists were at the time wearing striped uniforms and cooling their heels in jail following passage of the Edmunds Act of 1882.

So the bishop excommunicated George.

It wasn't a valid excommunication, by any means.[40] The bishop didn't follow standard procedure. Nor was the action recorded. Still, there it was. And George, never one to leave things alone, went public with his opposition by writing a play entitled *Celestial Marriage.*

The behavior and actions and attitudes of George Armstrong Hicks beg the question: how much is too much? When it comes right down to it, the Church had been extremely patient with George; even after all his railing against the *prophet*, for crying out loud, he was allowed to remain in the fold. But he didn't see it that way. For the next forty years, he "lived under the impression that he had been cut off, as he put it, 'for taking a stand against Polygamy and in favor of National Law.'"[41]

Justification can be an amusing thing.

So what happened to George Armstrong Hicks? Bitton poses an interesting question:

> One wonders whether during this time of discontent loyalty to his parents and parents-in-law came into play, whether he ever spoke out in defense of the church against its enemies, or whether there were tugs and pulls from his wife and children. Hicks himself was not ostracized.[42]

And there you have it. George himself was not ostracized. When the national political parties were established in Utah, he was unanimously elected chair of at least one Republican rally in Spanish Fork. He taught school. He was a justice of the peace and served as postmaster. He was a school trustee. He wrote articles for the local newspapers. He even gave a lecture at Brigham Young University. And, as mentioned, in 1913 he wrote a history of early Spanish Fork from his perspective as one who had lived that history.

At last, George Armstrong Hicks started to mellow. His beloved wife and companion, Betsy, died in 1922. There may not have been record of his second excommunication, but he was rebaptized anyway. Apostle Reed Smoot, also serving as a United States Senator, seems to have taken the initiative for the action, but at any rate it had the full support of the First Presidency. On June 25, 1923, at the Hotel Utah in Salt Lake City, Smoot "reconfirmed on George A. Hicks all his former blessings together with the restoration to him of the [priesthood] position of seventy in The Church of Jesus Christ of Latter-day Saints."[43]

On March 24, 1924, he was finally sealed to Betsy—by proxy—in the Salt Lake Temple.

The next year he was ordained a high priest.

And on June 30, 1926, he died—but not before "talking to a granddaughter and signing, in his shaky hand, the following statement: 'He has always been a firm believer in the Church of Jesus Christ of Latter-day Saints.'"[44]

If you're confused, you're not alone.

Did he finally doubt his doubts? Did that "doubt of doubt" cause him to want to be fully in the fold as his life ebbed to an end?

Perhaps the lines engraved on his headstone say it all. Under the title "George A. Hicks—Poet and Moralist" is this inscription:

No vicious creed perplexed his mind,
Nor brought misgivings to his breast.
He strove to love the human kind
And wished to all, both peace and rest.[45]

What we have here is, without question, a colorful character. For years he was what Bitton described as "a faultfinder, a complainer, a blamer." But we are also reminded that many of the early Saints went through the same experiences George did—and, says Bitton, "rather than stewing and fuming, nursing a sense of victimhood, fueling their bitterness by griping sessions with other malcontents, they maintained a different perspective, a different spirit."[46]

We see, as Bitton put it, as least three versions of George Armstrong Hicks: the enthusiast and believer, the cynic and critic, and the humble devotee. It seemed he was never of one mind, but we do know one thing: he may have enjoyed the label of *infidel*, but he didn't want to be seen as having gone off the deep end. As he himself put it:

I will say that with all my infidelity I have never lost faith in a glorious world beyond the grave where there is no death but I do not believe in any resurrection of the body but I believe in the immortality of the soul and in eternal progression. I also believe in future rewards and punishments.

I believe that a time will come when we will all
be judged according to the deeds done in the
body and that we will be classified according to
our intelligence.[47]

And don't worry . . . as we said earlier, if you're still confused,
you're not alone.

ABOUT THE AUTHOR

KATHRYN JENKINS GORDON LOVES HISTORY—ESPECIALLY Church history—and gets a real charge out of ferreting out its most colorful characters.

The managing editor at Covenant Communications, Inc., she has more than forty years of professional experience in corporate and internal communications, public relations, media relations, marketing communications, and publications management. She has been press secretary for a US Congressman; vice president of a Salt Lake City publishing company; manager of strategic communications for Novell, Inc.; director of public relations at a private college in Salt Lake City; and has held communications management positions at a variety of national and international corporations.

She is the author or coauthor of more than eight dozen published books and wrote an award-winning book-length poetry manuscript recognized by the governor of Utah. A former member of Sigma Delta Chi, she was named an Outstanding Young Woman of America.

Her interests include reading, writing, cooking, traveling, and doing family history. She has met five presidents of the United States, sailed up the Nile River, prayed in the Garden of Gethsemane, eaten tempura in Tokyo, and received a dozen long-stemmed red roses from a stranger on the street in Athens.

She and her husband, Glenn, parent a combined family of ten children and five (soon to be six) grandchildren.

ENDNOTES

James Strang

1 Doyle C. Fitzpatrick, *The King Strang Story: A Vindication of James J. Strang, the Beaver Island Mormon King* (Lansing: National Press, 1970), 21.

2 Henry E. Legler, *A Moses of the Mormons: Strang's City of Refuge and Island Kingdom*, Issues 15–16, 118.

3 Warren Post, "History of James Strang: The Birth and Parentage of the Prophet James," *StrangStudies.org*.

4 "Strang, the Man," *MormonBeliefs.com*.

5 Ibid.

6 Legler, 118–119.

7 Mark Strang, *The Diary of James J. Strang: Deciphered, Transcribed, Introduced, and Annotated* (East Lansing: Michigan State University Press, 1961), entry for March 21, 1832.

8 W. A. Titus, "Historic Spots in Wisconsin: Voree," *The Wisconsin Magazine of History*, Vol. 9, No. 4, July 1926, 435–436.

9 Fitzpatrick, *The King Strang Story*, 24.

10 D. Michael Quinn, "The Mormon Succession Crisis of 1844," *BYU Studies*, Vol. 016, No. 2, 195.

11 *Times and Seasons*, Vol. V., No. 16, September 2, 1844.

12 Legler, *A Moses of the Mormons*, 118–119.

13 Ardis E. Parshall, "James J. Strang to John Taylor and Orson Hyde, with Reply, 1846," *Keepapitchinin*, October 6, 2011.

14 Ibid.

15 Daniel C. Peterson, "Defending the Faith: The story behind James Strang and his sect," *Deseret News*, June 9, 2011.

16 *The Saints' Herald* 35 (December 29, 1888): 831–832.

17 Peterson.

18 Letter from Chauncy Loomis to Joseph Smith III, "Experience on Beaver Island with James J. Strang," *Saints' Herald*, Nov. 10, 1888, 718–719.

19 The following information from Letter from Chauncy Loomis to Joseph Smith III, as reported in Peterson.

20 Letter from Chauncy Loomis to Joseph Smith III.

Elizabeth Ann Claridge McCune

1 Celeste Tholen Rosenlof, "Voice from the Past: Elizabeth Claridge McCune," Aspiring Mormon Women Blog.

2 Carol Ann S. Van Wagoner, "Elizabeth Ann Claridge McCune: At Home on the Hill," In *Worth Their Salt: Notable But Often Unnoted Women of Utah*, ed. Colleen Whitley (Logan, Utah: Utah State University Press, 1996), 93.

3 Orson Feguson Whitney, *History of Utah* (Salt Lake City: G. Q. Cannon, 1904), 505.

4 Andrew Jensen, *Latter-Day Saint Biographical Encyclopedia* (Salt Lake City: A. Jenson History Co., 1920), 161.

5 Ibid.

6 Whitney.

7 Whitney, 505–506.

8 Whitney, 506.

9 Ibid.

10 Rosenlof.

11 Preston Nibley, "Elizabeth Claridge McCune One of Great Women of the Church," *Deseret News*, March 13, 1954.

12 Nibley.

13 Orvin Nebeker Malmquist, *The First 100 Years: A History of the 'Salt Lake Tribune,' 1871–1971* (Salt Lake City: Utah State Historical Society, 1971), 443.

14 Committee on Privileges and Elections, *In the Matter of the Protests Against the Right of Hon. Reed Smoot, A Senator From the State of Utah, to Hold His Seat.* Doc. No. 486. 59th Cong, 1st Sess. Committee on Privileges and Elections (United States Senate. Washington, D.C.: US Government Printing Office, 1906), 860.

15 Stuart Martin, *The Mystery of Mormonism* (London: Odhams, 1920), 213.

16 B. H. Roberts, *A Comprehensive History of the Church of Jesus Christ of Latter-Day Saints: Century I* (Salt Lake City: Deseret News Press, 1930), 344.

17 Susa Young Gates, "The Gardo House," *Improvement Era* 20 (1917):1099–1103; *Journal History of the Church of Jesus Christ of Latter-day Saints*, September 2, 1873 (microfilm, LDS Church Historical Department, Salt Lake City); Clarissa Young Spencer and Mabel Harmer, *Brigham Young at Home* (Salt Lake City: Deseret Book, 1972), 219–221.

18 Susa Young Gates, "Biographical Sketches, Elizabeth Claridge McCune," *Young Woman's Journal*, August 1898, 340.

19 Ibid.

20 "Golden Wedding of Mr. and Mrs. A. W. McCune," *Relief Society Magazine* 9 (August 1922):405.

21 "From Various Missionary Fields," *Millennial Star* 58 No. 35 (August 27, 1896): 555.

22 "London Conference," *Millennial Star* 59, No. 43 (October 28, 1897):684.

23 Gates, "Biographical Sketches," 342.

24 Gates, "Biographical Sketches," 343.

25 "Nottingham Conference," *Millennial Star* 59, No. 45 (November 11, 1897): 714–715.

26 "Our First Lady Missionaries," *Millennial Star* 60, No. 30 (July 28, 1898):472.

27 *Journal History of The Church of Jesus Christ of Latter-day Saints*, 11 March 1898.

28 Joseph W. McMurrin, "Lady Missionaries," *Young Woman's Journal* 15 (December 1904):539–540.

29 "Our First Lady Missionaries," *Millennial Star* 60, No. 30 (July 28, 1898):473.

30 "A Letter from Bristol," *Millennial Star* 60, No. 30 (July 28, 1898):476.

31 Gates, "Biographical Sketches," 339–343.

32 Rosenlof.

33 "Alfred W. McCune Mansion," Inventory—Nomination Form. National Register of Historic Places. National Park Service. US Department of the Interior, June 13, 1974.

34 Thomas G. Alexander, *Mormonism in Transition* (Urbana, Ill.: University of Illinois Press, 1996), 184.

35 This and other information regarding the "haunting" of the McCune Mansion from hauntedhouses.com.

Martin Harris

1 I am indebted to historian Ardis E. Parshall for the information in this chapter, which first appeared in her blog, *Keepapitchinin*, on September 17, 2012, under the title, "'Killed by Mistake': The Murder of Martin Harris, 1841." Parshall has a keen and unusual gift for ferreting out the most bizarre of events in Mormon history.

Clarissa Smith Williams

1 See Janet Peterson and LaRene Gaunt, *Faith, Hope, and Charity* (American Fork: Covenant Communications, Inc., 2008), 110–111.

2 Evalyn Darger Bennett, "Clarissa Williams," *Encyclopedia of Mormonism*, ed. Daniel H. Ludlow (Macmillan Publishing Company, 1992).

3 Bennett.

4 Bennett.

5 Ibid.

6 *Relief Society Magazine* 15 (Dec. 1928): 668–669.

7 Clarissa Smith Williams, in *Relief Society Magazine,* Dec. 1921, 696.

8 See Bennett; and Jill Mulvay Derr, Janath Russell Cannon, and Maureen Ursenbach Beecher, *Women of Covenant: The Story of Relief Society* (1992), 232–240.

9   Bennett.

10   "Stake Project Safeguards Mothers: Cottonwood Maternity Hospital Complete 26 Years," *Deseret News*, Nov. 8, 1950, 4.

11   "Stake Project Safeguards Mothers."

12   Ibid.

13   Ibid.

14   See Derr, Cannon, and Beecher, 231.

15   "Stake Project Safeguards Mothers."

16   All information about the wheat program taken from "Relief Society Wheat Project," LDS Women of God blog, August 22, 2008; taken from *Women of Covenant.*

17   Relief Society General Board Minutes, Apr. 4, 1922.

18   Information about the maternity chests and bundles taken from Ardis E. Parshall, "Relief Society Maternity Chests and Bundles, 1923," *Keepapitchinin*, June 2, 2015.

19   See October conference minutes, *Relief Society Magazine*, December 1923.

Olive Ann Oatman

1   Margot Mifflin, *The Blue Tattoo: The Life of Olive Oatman* (Lincoln: University of Nebraska Press, 2009).

2   I am indebted for this and much of the information about the Indian attack and its aftermath, including Olive's experiences with the Indians, to Robert B. Smith, who posted writing on history.net from an article that originally appeared in the August 2001 issue of *Wild West* entitled "Apache Captives' Ordeal."

3   Brian McGinty. *The Oatman Massacre: A Tale of Desert Captivity and Survival* (Norman, Oklahoma: University of Oklahoma Press, 2004), 85.

4   *The Tucson Citizen*, September 26, 1913.

5   Margot Mifflin, "Ten Myths About Olive Oatman," *True West Magazine*, August 1, 2009.

6   McGinty, 102.

7   Mifflin, "Ten Myths."

8   Mifflin, *Blue Tattoo*, 78.

9   Smith.

10 Ibid.

11 Ibid.

12 Mifflin, "Ten Myths."; Mifflin, *Blue Tattoo*, 88.

13 Smith.

14 Ibid.

15 Ibid.

16 Ibid.

17 Joan Swallow Reiter, "The Great Marriage Boom," *The Old West: The Women* (Canada: Littlehampton Book Services Ltd., 1978).

18 William B. Rice, "The Captivity of Olive Oatman: A Newspaper Account," *California Historical Society Quarterly*, Vol. 21, No. 2 (June 1942), 97–106.

19 Mifflin, "Ten Myths."

20 Ibid.

21 Brian McGinty, *The Oatman Massacre: A Tale of Desert Captivity and Survival*, 2004, 152; Richard H. Dillon. *Tragedy at Oatman Flat: Massacre, Captivity, Mystery*. American West 18, no. 2 (1981), 46–59.

22 Mifflin, "Ten Myths."

23 Mifflin, *Blue Tattoo*, 73–74.

24 McGinty, 176–177.

Other sources that contributed information include the Denison *Daily Herald*, April 25, 1907; the *New York Times*, May 4, 1858; Howard H. Peckham, *Captured by Indians: True Tales of Pioneer Survivors* (New Brunswick, New Jersey: Rutgers University Press, 1954); Edward J. Pettid, "The Oatman Story," *Arizona Highways*, November 1968; John Stanley, "Arizona Explained: Olive Oatman Had Eventual Life," *The Republic*, July 9, 2013; and Timoty Braatz, *Surviving Conquest* (Lincoln, Nebraska: University of Nebraska Press, 2003).

William Hooper Young

1 Todd Compton, "John Willard Young, Brigham Young, and the Development of Presidential Succession in the LDS Church," *Dialogue*, Vol. 35, No. 4 (Winter 2002).

2   Charles W. Watson, *John Willard Young and the 1887 Movement for Utah Statehood*, PhD Dissertation, Brigham Young University, Dept. of History, 1984.

3   Ibid.

4   Ardis E. Parshall, "Hooper Young's Murder of Anna Pulitzer," *Keepapitchinin* blog, August 14, 2010. I am indebted to historian Ardis Parshall for much of the information that contributed to this chapter. In addition to this blog, she also presented "William Hooper Young and the Murder of Anna Pulitzer," at the Sunstone Symposium in Salt Lake City, Utah, in August 2003, and wrote "Living History: From Cowboy to Killer: A Utah Boy's Story" in the *Salt Lake Tribune*, both of which were consulted for information adapted in this chapter.

5   Parshall, "Hooper Young's Murder."

6   Ibid.

7   This and the rest of McQuarrie's conversation with Hooper from Parshall, "Hooper Young's Murder."

8   Ibid.

9   Information about the missionaries' actions is adapted from Parshall, "Living History."

10 Parshall, "Hooper Young's Murder."

11 Ibid.

12 Ibid.

Isaac Perry Decker

1   This incident is taken from details in Karl Decker, "LeRay Decker's Story," in Stevens Call Nelson, *Legacy Builders: The Story of LeRay Decker, His Wife, and Their Progenitors*, [Provo, UT: 2007], 51.

2   Ibid.

3   Information on the measles epidemic is taken from Amy Tanner Thiriot, "'Take Care of the Children': The 1869 Salt Lake City Measles Epidemic," *Keepapitchinin*, February 11, 2015.

Eli N. Pace

1   John Krakauer, *Under the Banner of Heaven: A Story of Violent Faith* (New York: Random House, Inc., 2003), 236.

2   Wayne Atilio Capurro, *White Flag: America's First 9/11* (Bloomington, IN: AuthorHouse, 2007), 328.

3   Krakauer, 236.

4   Ibid.

5   Capurro, 328.

6   Vern Anderson, "Did Murders Happen in Mormon Ward? 1883 Letter May Solve Mystery of Trio," *Salt Lake Tribune*, Nov. 28, 1993, B3.

7   Capurro, 329.

8   Information about what happened next taken from Capurro, 329–330.

9   Capurro, 330.

10   Ibid.

11   Krakauer, 238.

12   Anderson.

13   Krakauer, 238.

14   Krakauer, 239.

15   Information about these stories provided by Krakauer, 239–240.

16   Krakauer, 240.

17   The letter was first published by the Southeastern Utah Society of Arts and Sciences, Inc., in an article by Wesley Larsen, "The 'Letter' or Were the Powell Men Really Killed by Indians?" *Canyon Legacy*, Spring 1993.

18   Anderson.

19   John D. Lee diary, 19 Jan. 1870, in Robert Glass Cleland and Juanita Brooks, *A Mormon Chronicle: The Diaries of John D. Lee, 1848–1876* (Huntington Library Press, 2004), 2:133–134.

20   D. Michael Quinn, *Mormon Hierarchy: Extensions of Power* (Salt Lake City, Utah: Signature Books, 1997), 534.

Julia Murdock Smith Dixon Middleton

1   Sunny McClellan Morton, "On Being Adopted: Julia Murdock Smith," *Dialogue*, Vol. 36, No. 4 (Winter 2003), 181.

2   Biographical information from Sunny McClellan Morton, "The Forgotten Daughter: Julia Murdock Smith," *Mormon Historical Studies*, Vol. 3, No. 2 (Fall 2002), 35–60.

3   Ibid.

4   Ibid., 37–38.

5   Morton, "The Forgotten Daughter."

6   Ibid.; and John Murdock, "Autobiography," microfilm. Historical Department of The Church of Jesus Christ of Latter-day Saints, Salt Lake City, Utah, 148–149.

7   John Murdock, "A Synopsis of My History," Typescript, Historical Department of The Church of Jesus Christ of Latter-day Saints, Salt Lake City, Utah, 168.

8   Morton, "On Being Adopted."

9   Ibid.

10 Ibid.

11 Julie Berebitsky, *Like Our Very Own. Adoption and the Changing Culture of Motherhood, 1851–1950* (Lawrence, KS: University Press of Kansas, 2000).

12 Ibid.

13 Morton, "The Forgotten Daughter."

14 Ibid.

15 Betty Jean Lifton, *Journey of the Adopted Self: A Quest for Wholeness* (New York: BasicBooks, 1994), 48–49.

16 Morton, "The Forgotten Daughter."

17 Ibid.; and John Murdock, "Autobiography," 141.

18 Morton, "The Forgotten Daughter."

19 Ibid.

20 Ibid.

21 Ibid.

22 Ibid.

23 *Nauvoo Independent*, September 17, 1880.

24 Morton, "The Forgotten Daughter."

25 Ibid.

26 The dates and details of Julia's temple work are from Morton, "The Forgotten Daughter."

Andrew Balfour Hepburn and James Marsden

1   Ardis E. Parshall, "'A Disturbance at the Mormonite Chapel': 19th Century British Hooliganism and the Latter-day Saints," *Keepapitchinin*, June 10, 2013. You can find Ardis's blog at http://www.keepapitchinin.org, and it's well worth the trip!

2   Helen Marr Whitney, "Scenes in Nauvoo, and Incidents from H. C. Kimball's Journal," *Women's Exponent*, 12 (15 October 1883):74.

3   Letter to Heber C. Kimball, LDS Church collection.

4   Journal of William H. Kimball, Church collection, as contained in Jill C. Major, "William Henry Kimball and James Marsden: History of William Warner Major."

5   This and other discrepancies/corrections from Major, "William Henry Kimball and James Marsden: History of William Warner Major."

6   Harvey B. Black, *Early Members of the Reorganized Church of Jesus Christ of Latter-day Saints*, 3:31; and Willard Richards Journal, 19 April 1844, LDS Church Archives.

7   Parshall.

8   Andrew Balfour Hepburn, *Mormonism Exploded, or, The Religion of the Latter-day Saints Proved to Be a System of Imposture, Blasphemy and Immorality with the Autobiography and Portrait of the Author. In Two Parts. Part 1 by A.B. Hepburn, an Anti-Mormon Lecturer.*

9   This and other pieces of Andrew's story from Parshall.

10 Information about missionary harassment taken from Parshall.

11 Parshall.

12 Ibid.

Marvel Farrell Andersen

1   Basic biographical information taken from Marvel Farrell Andersen's obituary, *Deseret News*, February 26, 1991.

2   Much of the information for this chapter was adapted from Ardis E. Parshall, "The Chapel Built by Cigarettes," *Keepapitchinin*, October 12, 2008. Parhsall, a renowned Mormon historian,

has dedicated a career to ferreting out little-known and highly fascinating pieces of Mormon history.

3   Richard O. Cowan, "From the Battlefield to the Vatican to the Classroom: The Story of Eldin Ricks," BYU Religious Studies Center website.

Mary Ann Angell Young

1   Louise Maunsell Field, "The Spinster Looks at Marriage," *The North American Review*, Vol. 232, No. 6 (1931), 552–558.

2   I am indebted for much of the information in this chapter to Rex G. Jensen, "Mary Ann Angell Young," *Ensign*, July 1993.

3   Kate B. Carter, comp., *Our Pioneer Heritage,* 20 vols., (Salt Lake City: Daughters of Utah Pioneers, 1958–77), 16:53.

4   Emmeline B. Wells, "Biography of Mary Ann Angell Young," *Juvenile Instructor,* 1 Jan. 1891, 17.

5   Wells, 17.

6   Leonard J. Arrington, *Brigham Young: American Moses* (New York: Alfred A. Knopf, 1985), 37.

7   Arrington, 61.

8   Wells, 19.

9   *History of the Church,* 3:23.

10 Wells, 56.

11 Wells, 57.

12 Elden J. Watson, ed., *Manuscript History of Brigham Young, 1802–1844* (Salt Lake City: Smith Secretarial Service, 1968), 125.

13 Wells, 94.

14 Wells, 95.

15 Emmeline B. Wells, "L.D.S. Women of the Past," *Woman's Exponent,* vol. 36, no. 9 (May 1908), 66.

Orson Pratt Jr.

1   I am indebted for most of the information in this chapter to Richard S. and Mary C. Van Wagoner, "Orson Pratt, Jr.: Gifted Son of an Apostle and an Apostate," *Dialogue,* Vol. 21, No. 1.

2   James G. Bleak, "Annals of the Southern Utah Mission," Book A, n.d., Typescript in Special Collections, Harold B. Lee Library, Brigham Young University, Provo, Utah.

3   Milando Pratt, "Life and Labors of Orson Pratt," *The Contributor* 12 (1891):393.

4   Endowment House Records, No. 738, Book A, cited on Orson Pratt, Jr., Family Group Sheet, LDS Genealogical Society, Salt Lake City.

5   Salt Lake Stake Record of Baptisms and Rebaptisms, 1847–63, microfilm.

6   H. Dean Garrett, "Rebaptism," *Encyclopedia of Mormonism*, ed. Daniel H. Ludlow (New York: Macmillan Publishing Company, 1992).

7   "Orson Pratt's Harem," *New York Herald*, 18 May 1877, New York City Public Library, 2.

8   *Anti-Polygamy Standard*, 11 [February 1882]: 81.

9   *Millennial Star*, 18:784.

10   *Deseret News*, 4 April 1857.

11   *Deseret News*, 28 June 1857.

12   "Orson Pratt's Harem," 2.

13   Journal History of the Church, 24 February 1856.

14   Bleak, 175.

15   Bleak, 172–175.

16   *Deseret News*, Dec. 7, 1903, 10.

George Armstrong Hicks

1   I am deeply indebted to Davis Bitton for his masterful article, "'I'd Rather Have Some Roasting Ears': The Peregrinations of George Armstrong Hicks," *Utah Historical Quarterly*, Vol. 68, No. 3 (Summer 2000):196–222, from which much of the information for this chapter was adapted.

2   Bitton, 196.

3   Polly Aird, "George Armstrong Hicks: Dixie Mormon/Voice of Dissent," *Keepapitchinin*, May 23, 2011.

4   Bitton, 196.

5   Bitton, 197.

6   Family Record and History of George Armstrong Hicks (privately printed: Kerry J. Zabriskie, 1995), 9. Hereafter cited as Hicks.

7   Bitton, 199.

8   Ibid.

9   Hicks, 9.

10   Hicks, 11.

11   Hicks, 12. For more information on similar episodes, see Kenneth W. Godfrey, "Crime and Punishment in Mormon Nauvoo, 1839–1846," *BYU Studies* 32 (Winter-Spring 1992):195–227.

12   Hicks, 12.

13   Hicks, 13.

14   Bitton, 204.

15   Hicks, 20. For more information about the settlement, see also Elisha Warner, *The History of Spanish Fork* (Spanish Fork, UT: Press Publishing Company, 1930), 34–50.

16   George A. Hicks, "History of Spanish Fork," 4, typescript, Special Collections, Harold B. Lee Library, Brigham Young University.

17   Hicks, 20.

18   Hicks, 29. For more information, see Davis Bitton and Linda P. Wilcox, "Pestiferous Ironclads: The Grasshopper Problem in Pioneer Utah," *Utah Historical Quarterly* 46 (Fall 1978):335–355.

19   Bitton, 205.

20   Hicks, 20–21. "Apostle Smith made wonderful predictions in regard to the future and greatness of Palmyra, which, to put it mildly, never materialized"; Hicks, "History of Spanish Fork."

21   Hicks, 21.

22   Bitton, 206.

23   Hicks, "History of Spanish Fork," 13.

24   Hicks, 41–42.

25   Hicks, "History of Spanish Fork," 10.

26   Bitton, 207.

27   Bitton, 210.

28   Bitton, 211.

29   Bitton, 212.

30   Hicks, 50.

31   Hicks, 52.

32 See other verses in Thomas E. Cheney, *Mormon Songs from the Rocky Mountains: A Compilation of Mormon Folksongs* (Austin, University of Texas Press, 1968), 118–120.

33 Andrew Karl Larson, "I Was Called to Dixie," (privately published, 1961; reprinted St. George, Utah: Dixie College Foundation, 1993), 76. See also *Our Pioneer Heritage* 1 (1964):595.

34 Hicks, 57; Bitton, 214.

35 George A. Hicks to Brigham Young, December 4, 1868; Edyth Romney transcription in possession of the Joseph Fielding Smith Institute for Latter-day Saint History (Smith Institute), Brigham Young University.

36 Bitton, 215. For different versions of this song, see Cheney, *Mormon Songs*, 200–205; Austin E. Fife, "Mountain Meadows Massacre," *Western Folklore* 12 (October 1953):229–237; and Lester A. Hubbard, *Ballads and Songs from Utah* (Salt Lake City: University of Utah Press, 1961), 445.

37 Bitton, 215.

38 Robert Glass Cleland and Juanita Brooks, eds., *A Mormon Chronicle: The Diaries of John D. Lee, 1848– 1876*, 2 vols. (San Marino, CA: Huntington Library, 1955), 2:100–102, entry for April 11 [12], 1868.

39 Cleland and Brooks, 2:122–23, entry for July 4, 1869.

40 Bitton, 218.

41 Bitton, 218; and Undated letter to Bishop Ralph D. Morgan, "Scrap Book Kept By Geo A. Hicks For Amusement and Future Reference," microfilm, LDS Church Archives, hereafter identified as Scrap Book.

42 Bitton, 218.

43 This and following information on Hicks's later activities taken from Bitton, 219.

44 Reed Smoot to George A. Hicks, June 22, 1923, and Reed Smoot to Joseph Reece, Payson, Utah, June 25, 1923, Scrap Book.

45 Bitton, 219; signed statement in possession of Mrs. Jean Groberg, a granddaughter.

46 Bitton, 220.

47 Bitton, 221.
48 Hicks, 42.